John L. Girardeau

Instrumental Music in the Public Worship of the Church

John L. Girardeau

Instrumental Music in the Public Worship of the Church

ISBN/EAN: 9783337290177

Printed in Europe, USA, Canada, Australia, Japan

Cover: Foto ©Thomas Meinert / pixelio.de

More available books at **www.hansebooks.com**

INSTRUMENTAL MUSIC

IN THE

PUBLIC WORSHIP OF THE CHURCH.

INSTRUMENTAL MUSIC

IN THE

PUBLIC WORSHIP

OF

THE CHURCH.

BY

JOHN L. GIRARDEAU,

PROFESSOR IN COLUMBIA THEOLOGICAL SEMINARY, SOUTH CAROLINA.

RICHMOND, VA.:
WHITTET & SHEPPERSON, PRINTERS, 1001 MAIN STREET.
1888.

PREFACE.

The following treatise owes its origin to a desire expressed by members of the last Senior Class in Columbia Theological Seminary to hear a discussion of the question whether instrumental music may be legitimately used in the public worship of the Church. Possessed of deep convictions on that subject, the writer could not refuse compliance with such a request, and accordingly delivered a course of lectures to the class. A dear Christian friend, who heard one of these lectures preached as a sermon, suggested the propriety of their being published, and being aware that the writer was not encumbered with a superfluity of this world's goods, generously tendered the means to render the suggestion practical. Although cautioned that she might make a useless pecuniary sacrifice, as the current of the Church's views is now set in a direction opposed to the doctrine of the treatise, she insisted upon executing her intention, on the ground that she would contribute to erect a testimony to the truth. Hence the appearance of this little book before the public.

It will, no doubt, be said that the attempt to prove the unjustifiable employment of instrumental music in the public worship of the Church is schismatical, since the practice is now well-nigh universal; that it is trivial, inasmuch as it concerns a mere circumstantial in the services of religion; and that it is useless, as the tendency which is resisted is invincible, and is destined to triumph throughout Protestant Christendom. To all this one answer alone is offered, and it is sufficient, namely: that the attempt is grounded in truth. It involves a contest for a mighty and all-comprehending principle, by opposing one of the special forms in which it is now commonly transcended and violated. It is that principle, emphasized in the following remarks as scriptural and regulative, that lends importance to the discussion, and redeems it from the reproach of being narrow and trifling.

The argument is commended to the consideration of any of God's people into whose hands it may fall; but it is especially addressed to Presbyterians, to whose venerable standards, as well as directly to the Scriptures, the appeal for proof is taken. They are entreated to read it, and to render judgment according to the evidence submitted. May that Almighty Spirit, whose illumination our divine Lord and Saviour promised to his followers, guide each reader to the truth!

COLUMBIA, S. C.

CONTENTS.

	PAGE.
THE QUESTION STATED,	9
I. GENERAL ARGUMENT FROM SCRIPTURE,	9
II. ARGUMENT FROM THE OLD TESTAMENT,	27
III. ARGUMENT FROM THE NEW TESTAMENT,	80
IV. ARGUMENT FROM THE PRESBYTERIAN STANDARDS,	123
V. HISTORICAL ARGUMENT,	155
VI. ARGUMENTS IN FAVOR OF INSTRUMENTAL MUSIC CONSIDERED,	180
VII. CONCLUDING REMARKS,	200

INSTRUMENTAL MUSIC

IN THE

PUBLIC WORSHIP OF THE CHURCH.

In the discussion of the question, Whether the use of instrumental music in the worship of the church is permissible or not, it must be premised:

First, that the question *is not* in regard to private or family worship, or to that of social gatherings which are not ecclesiastical in their nature, nor with reference to the utility or tastefulness of instrumental music, nor in relation to the abuse to which it may be liable; but,

Secondly, the question *is* precisely, Is the use of instrumental music in the public worship of the church *justifiable?* The design of this discussion is, with the help of the divine Spirit, to prove the negative.

I.

THE GENERAL ARGUMENT FROM SCRIPTURE.

Attention, at the outset, is invoked to the considerations which serve to establish the following controlling principle: A divine warrant is necessary for every element of doctrine, government and worship in the church; that is, whatsoever in these spheres is not commanded in the Scriptures, either expressly or by good and necessary consequence from their statements, *is forbidden.*

1. This principle is deducible by logical inference from the great truth—confessed by Protestants—that the Scriptures are an infallible rule of faith and practice, and therefore supreme, perfect and sufficient for all the needs of the Church. "All Scripture is given by inspiration of God, and is profitable for doctrine, for reproof, for correction, for instruction in righteousness: that the man of God may be perfect, thoroughly furnished unto all good works." This truth operates positively to the inclusion of everything in the doctrine, government and worship of the church which is commanded, explicitly or implicitly, in the Scriptures, and negatively to the exclusion of everything which is not so commanded.

2. This principle of the necessity of a divine warrant for everything in the faith and practice of the church is proved by didactic statements of Scripture.

Num. xv. 39, 40: "Remember all the commandments of the Lord and do them; and that ye seek not after your own heart and your own eyes, after which ye use to go a whoring: that ye may remember and do all my commandments, and be holy unto your God." Ex. xxv. 40: "And look that thou make them after their pattern, which was showed thee in the mount." Heb. viii. 5: "Who serve unto the example and shadow of heavenly things, as Moses was admonished of God, when he was about to make the tabernacle: for, See, saith he, that thou make all things according to the pattern showed to thee in the mount." Deut. iv. 2: "Ye shall not add unto the word which I command you, neither shall ye diminish aught from it, that ye may keep the commandments of the Lord your God which I command you." Deut. xii. 32: "What thing soever I command you, observe to do it: thou shalt not add thereto, nor diminish from it." Prov. xxx. 5, 6: "Every word of God is pure: he is a shield unto them that put their trust in him. Add thou not unto his words, lest he reprove thee, and thou be found a liar." Isa. viii. 20: "To the law and to the testimony: if they speak not according to this word, it is because there is no light in them." Dan. ii. 44: "And in the days of these kings shall the God of heaven set up a kingdom, which shall never be destroyed: and the kingdom shall not be left to other people." Matt. xv. 6: "Thus have ye made the commandment of God of none effect by your tradition." Matt. xxviii. 19, 20: "Go ye, therefore, and teach all nations, baptizing them in the name of the Father, and of the Son, and of the Holy Ghost: teaching them to observe all things whatsoever I have commanded you." Col. ii. 20 23: "Wherefore if ye be dead with Christ from the rudiments of the world, why, as though living in the world, are ye subject to ordinances, (touch not; taste not; handle not; which are all to perish with the using;) after the commandments and doctrines of men? which things have indeed a shew of wisdom in will-worship, and humility, and neglecting of the body; not in any honor to the satisfying of the flesh." 2 Tim. iii. 16, 17: "All scripture is given by inspiration of God, and is profitable for doctrine, for reproof, for correction, for instruction in righteousness: that the man of God may be perfect, thoroughly furnished unto all good works." Rev. xxii. 18, 19: "For I testify unto every man that heareth the words of the prophecy of this book, If any man shall add unto these things, God shall add unto him the plagues that are written in this book: and if any man shall take away from the words of the book of this prophecy, God shall take away his part out of the book of life, and out of the holy city, and out of the things which are written in this book."

These solemn statements and awful warnings teach us the lesson, that to introduce any devices and inventions of our own into the doctrine, government or worship of the church, is to add to the words of God, and to fail in maintaining the principles and truths, or in complying with the institutions and ordinances, delivered to us in the Scriptures, is to take away from the words of God. The Romanists, for example, who hold the doctrine of transubstantiation, and observe the sacrifice of the mass, add to God's words; and the Quakers, who maintain the co-ordinate authority of immediate revelations of new, original truth with the inspired Oracles, and neglect the observance of the sacraments, both add to and take away from them. And, in like manner, those who import instrumental music into the ordained worship of the New Testament Church transcend the warrant of Scripture, and add to the words which Christ our Lord has commanded.

3. There are concrete instances recorded in the Scriptures which graphically illustrate the same great principle.

(1.) Gen. iv: Cain and his offering. The brothers, Cain and Abel, had been in childhood beyond all doubt instructed by their parents in the knowledge of the first promise of redemption to be accomplished by atonement. They had, we have every reason to believe, often seen their father offering animal sacrifices in the worship of God. To this mode of worship they had been accustomed. Cain, the type of rationalists and fabricators of rites and ceremonies in the house of the Lord, consulted his own wisdom and taste, and ventured to offer in God's worship the fruit of the ground—an unbloody sacrifice; while Abel, conforming to the appointments and prescribed usages in which he had been trained, expressed his faith and obedience by offering a lamb. Abel's worship was accepted and Cain's rejected. "And in process of time it came to pass, that Cain brought of the fruit of the ground an offering unto the Lord. And Abel, he also brought of the firstlings of his flock and of the fat thereof. And the Lord had respect unto Abel and to his offering; but unto Cain and his offering he had not respect." Thus, in the immediate family of Adam, we behold a signal and typical instance of self-assertion and disregard of divine prescriptions in the matter of worship. This was swiftly followed by God's disapprobation, and then came the development of sin in the atrocious crime of fratricide, and the banishment of the murderer from the communion of his family and the presence of his God.

(2.) Lev. x. 1–3: Nadab and Abihu. "And Nadab and Abihu, the sons of Aaron, took either of them his censer, and put fire therein, and put incense thereon, and offered strange fire before the Lord, which he commanded them not.[1] And there went out fire from the Lord, and devoured them, and they died before the Lord. Then Moses said unto Aaron, This is it that the

---

[1] That is, which he did not command them.

Lord spake, saying, I will be sanctified in them that come nigh me, and before all the people I will be glorified. And Aaron held his peace." These young men, as the sons of Israel's high priest, were legitimately employed in discharging the appointed functions of the sacerdotal office. But they presumed to add to God's commandments. Exercising their own will in regard to the mode of his worship, they did that which he did not command them, and they were instantly killed for their wicked temerity.

(3.) Num. xvi.: Korah, Dathan and Abiram. God had consecrated those descendants of Levi who sprang from Aaron to the priesthood, while the remaining descendants of Levi were set apart to other offices pertaining to the service of the tabernacle. Korah was a Levite, but not a son of Aaron. Dathan and Abiram were not even Levites, but appear to have descended from Reuben. When, therefore, these men, asserting the claim that the whole congregation were entitled to rank with Moses and Aaron, ventured to assume to themselves functions which God had restricted to a certain class, they were overtaken by the swift indignation of Jehovah, and perished in an awful manner. "The ground clave asunder that was under them; and the earth opened her mouth, and swallowed them up, and their houses, and all the men that appertained unto Korah, and all their goods. They, and all that appertained unto them, went down alive into the pit, and the earth closed upon them: and they perished from among the congregation."

(4.) Num. xx.: Moses smiting the rock at Kadesh. When, on a previous occasion, the Israelites were suffering from thirst, God commanded Moses to smite the rock at Horeb. This he did, and water gushed forth abundantly. The apostle Paul tells us that that rock typified Christ. The typical teaching furnished by Moses, then, was that from the one death of Christ under the smiting of the law the grace of the Holy Ghost should proceed to satisfy the thirst of the soul. Christ was to be smitten unto death only once. Now again, at Kadesh, the Israelites suffer for want of water. God commands Moses to *speak* unto the rock. To this explicit command he rashly ventured to add. He spoke to the people, instead of the rock, and he *smote* the rock and smote it twice. He used his own judgment, asserted his own will, and taught the people falsely. For this sin he and Aaron, who concurred with him in its commission, were excluded from entrance into the promised land. "And the Lord spake unto Moses, saying, Take the rod, and gather thou the assembly together, thou and Aaron thy brother, and speak ye to the rock before their eyes; and it shall give forth his water, and thou shalt bring forth to them water out of the rock: so thou shalt give the congregation and their beasts drink. And Moses took the rod from before the Lord, as he commanded him. And Moses and Aaron gathered the congregation together before the rock, and he said unto them, Hear now, ye rebels; must we fetch you water out of this rock? And Moses lifted up his hand, and with his rod he smote the rock twice: and the water came out abundantly, and the congregation drank, and their beasts also. And the Lord spake unto Moses and Aaron, Because ye believed me not, to sanctify me in the eyes of the children of Israel, therefore ye shall not bring this congregation into the land which I have given them."

We have here an inexpressibly affecting instance of the sin and folly of adding human inventions to the ordinances of God's appointment, of the dreadful results that may follow from what men may conceive slight departures from obedience to the commands of God. Not to speak of Aaron, the accomplished orator, the venerable saint, the first anointed high priest of his people, this incomparable man, Moses, in whom were blended all natural gifts and supernatural graces, the deliverer, the legislator, the historian, the poet, the judge and the commander of Israel, after having brought them out of Egypt, conducted them through the parted waters of the Red Sea, mediated between them and God amidst the terrors of Sinai, led them through the horrors of the waste and howling desert,—this glorious man, now in sight of the Jordan, which like a thread separated them from the long-sought, long-coveted goal of their hearts, is doomed, for one addition to God's command, which no doubt seemed to him but a slight deviation from his instructions, to die short of the promised land.

(5.) 1 Sam. xiii.: Saul offering a burnt-offering at Gilgal. The king had no command to officiate as priest. Saul added to God's command and performed a function for which he had no authority. The circumstances seemed to him to justify the act. But he gained the divine disapprobation and lost his kingdom for the blunder. "As for Saul, he was yet in Gilgal, and all the people followed him trembling. And he tarried seven days, according to the set time that Samuel had appointed: but Samuel came not to Gilgal; and the people were scattered from him. And Saul said, Bring hither a burnt-offering to me, and peace-offerings. And he offered the burnt-offering. And it came to pass, that as soon as he had made an end of offering the burnt-offering, behold, Samuel came; and Saul went out to meet him that he might salute him. And Samuel said, What hast thou done? And Saul said, Because I saw that the people were scattered from me, and that thou camest not within the days appointed, and that the Philistines gathered themselves together at Michmash; therefore said I, The Philistines will come down now upon me to Gilgal, and I have not made supplication unto the Lord: I forced myself therefore, and offered a burnt-offering. And Samuel said to Saul, Thou hast done foolishly: thou hast not kept the commandment of the Lord thy God which he commanded thee: for now would the Lord have established thy kingdom upon Israel forever. But now thy kingdom shall not continue: the Lord hath sought him a man after his own heart, and the Lord hath commanded him to be captain over his people, because thou hast not kept that which the Lord commanded thee."

(G.) 1 Chron. xiii. 7, 8; xv. 11-15: Uzza and the ark, and David's subsequent obedience. The Levites, or, more particularly, the Kohathites, were expressly commanded to bear the ark. The manner of bearing it was also commanded. Rings were appended, through which staves were run. These poles, covered with gold, were to be supported on the shoulders of the bearers. They were forbidden to touch the ark upon pain of death. "After that, the sons of Kohath shall come to bear it: but they shall not touch any holy thing, lest they die." Such was God's command. In transporting it from the house of Abinadab, David infringed the divine command by directing the ark to be borne on a cart drawn by oxen. Then when the animals stumbled, Uzza, with the intention of saving the ark from falling, touched it with his hand. He was instantly killed for his pious disobedience. "And they carried the ark of God in a new cart out of the house of Abinadab: and Uzza and Ahio drave the cart. And David and all Israel played before God with all their might, and with singing, and with harps, and with psalteries, and with timbrels, and with cymbals, and with trumpets. And when they came unto the threshing-floor of Chidon, Uzza put forth his hand to hold the ark; for the oxen stumbled. And the anger of the Lord was kindled against Uzza, and he smote him, because he put his hand to the ark: and there he died before God." The offence was the more inexcusable, because the staves were never detached from the ark, and it is not at all likely that the Philistines, who had been subjected to so severe a treatment while they had it in their possession, had ventured to steal them. And it deserves consideration that those heathen had not been killed for handling the ark, while for doing the same thing God's people, who should have known better, were taught an awful lesson.

The magnificent demonstration suffered a disastrous arrest, and the king of Israel, sobered by the warning he had received, returned home to do what he ought to have done before—to study the law of God. Having accomplished this neglected office, he makes a second attempt to remove the sacred symbol of God's covenant to Jerusalem, but in a different fashion from the former. Let us hear the record. "And David called for Zadok and Abiathar the priests, and for the Levites, for Uriel, Asaiah, and Joel, Shemaiah, and Eliel and Amminadab, and said unto them, Ye are the chief of the fathers of the Levites: sanctify yourselves, both ye and your brethren, that ye may bring up the ark of the Lord God of Israel unto the place that I have prepared for it. For because ye did it not at the first, the Lord our God made a breach upon us, for that we sought him not after the due order. So the priests and the Levites sanctified themselves to bring up the ark of the Lord God of Israel. And the children of the Levites bare the ark upon their shoulders with the staves thereon, as Moses commanded according to the word of the Lord." It merits notice that when the ark was to be removed and instated in its place in the temple which was about to be dedicated, Solomon caused the "due order" to be observed. "And all the elders of Israel came; and the Levites took up the ark. And they brought up the ark, and the tabernacle of the congregation, and all the holy vessels that were in the tabernacle, these did the priests and the Levites bring up. . . . And the priests brought in the ark of the covenant of the Lord unto his place." [1] The history of this matter enforces the impressive lesson that we are not at liberty to use our own judgment and to act without a divine warrant in regard to things of God's appointment.

---

[1] 2 Chron. v. 4, 5, 7.

(7.) 2 Chron. xxvi. 16–21: King Uzziah officiating as a priest. God had given no warrant to a king to act as priest, and Uzziah arrogantly undertook, without such warrant, to discharge sacerdotal functions. The consequences of his impiety are vividly depicted in the following record: "But when he was strong, his heart was lifted up to his destruction: for he transgressed against the Lord his God, and went into the temple of the Lord to burn incense upon the altar of incense. And Azariah the priest went in after him, and with him fourscore priests of the Lord, that were valiant men: and they withstood Uzziah the king, and said unto him, It appertaineth not unto thee, Uzziah, to burn incense unto the Lord, but to the priests, the sons of Aaron, that are consecrated to burn incense: go out of the sanctuary; for thou hast trespassed; neither shall it be for thine honor from the Lord God. Then Uzziah was wroth, and had a censer in his hand to burn incense: and while he was wroth with the priests, the leprosy even rose up in his forehead before the priests in the house of the Lord, from beside the incense altar. And Azariah the chief priest, and all the priests, looked upon him, and behold, he was leprous in his forehead, and they thrust him out from thence, yea, himself hasted also to go out, because the Lord had smitten him. And Uzziah the king was a leper unto the day of his death, and dwelt in a several house, being a leper; for he was cut off from the house of the Lord."

(8.) 2 Chron. xxviii. 3–5: King Ahaz doubly offending as to function and place. He performed priestly functions without a divine warrant, and performed them in places which God had not appointed. For this wicked self-assertion he was visited with divine vengeance. "Moreover he burnt incense in the valley of the son of Hinnom, and burnt his children in the fire, after the abominations of the heathen whom the Lord had cast out before the children of Israel. He sacrificed also and burnt incense in the high places, and on the hills, and under every green tree. Wherefore the Lord his God delivered him into the hands of the king of Syria; and they smote him, and carried away a great multitude of them captives, and brought them to Damascus. And he was also delivered into the hands of the king of Israel, who smote him with a great slaughter."

(9.) The jealousy of God for the principle of a divine warrant for everything in his worship is most conspicuously illustrated in New Testament times, by the tremendous judgments which befell the Jewish people for perpetuating, without such a warrant, the typical ritual of the temple-service. Until the great atoning sacrifice was offered, they had a positive warrant from God for the observance of that order. But when that sacrifice had been offered, the veil of the temple had been rent in twain, and the Holy Ghost had been copiously poured out at the inauguration of a new dispensation, the positive warrant for the temple-worship was withdrawn. This Stephen insisted on before the Council, and the illustrious witness for Christ was murdered for his testimony. He charged that when their fathers had no warrant to worship sacrificially except at the temple they had persisted in observing that worship elsewhere; and now that God had withdrawn the warrant to worship at the temple, they demanded the right to worship there. "Ye do always," said the glorious servant of Jesus, "resist the Holy Ghost." For this sin, by which they endorsed their rejection of their Messiah and Saviour, their church-state and national polity were demolished, and they, after the experience of an unparalleled tribulation, were scattered to the four winds of heaven. Have we not the evidence before us at this day?

The mighty principle has thus been established, by an appeal to the didactic statements of God's word, and to special instances recorded in scriptural history, that a divine warrant is required for everything in the faith and practice of the Church, that whatsoever is not in the Scriptures commanded, either explicitly or by good and necessary consequence, is forbidden. The special application of this principle to the worship of God, as illustrated in the concrete examples which have been furnished, cannot escape the least attentive observation. God is seen manifesting a most vehement jealousy in protecting the purity of his worship. Any attempt to assert the judgment, the will, the taste of man apart from the express warrant of his Word, and to introduce into his worship human inventions, devices and methods, was overtaken by immediate retribution and rebuked by the thunderbolts of his wrath. Nor need we wonder at this; for the service which the creature professes to render to God reaches its highest and most formal expression in the worship which is offered him. In this act the majesty of the Most High is directly confronted. The worshipper presents himself face to face with the infinite Sovereign of heaven and earth, and assumes to lay at his feet the sincerest homage of the heart. In the performance of such an act to violate divine appointments or transcend divine prescription, to affirm the reason of a sinful creature against the wisdom, the will of a sinful creature against the authority, of God, is deliberately to flaunt an insult in his face, and to hurl an indignity against his throne. What else could follow but the flash of divine indignation? It is true that in the New Testament dispensation the same swift and visible arrest of this sin is not the ordinary rule. But the patience and forbearance of God can constitute no justification of its commission. Its punishment, if it be not repented of, is only deferred. "Because sentence against an evil work is not executed speedily, therefore the heart of the sons of men is fully set in them to do evil;" while the delayed justice of God is gathering to itself indignation to burst forth like an overwhelming tempest in the dreadful day of wrath.

The principle that has been emphasized is in direct opposition to that maintained by Romanists and Prelatists, and I regret to say by lax Presbyterians, that what is not forbidden in the Scriptures is permitted. The Church of England, in her twentieth article, concedes to the church "a power to decree rites and ceremonies," with this limitation alone upon its exercise, "that it is not lawful for the church to ordain anything that is contrary to God's written word."[1] The princi-

---

[1] Some curious and remarkable statements have been made with reference to this article. When, in 1808, the question of the introduction of instrumental music into public worship was before the Presbytery of Glasgow, the Rev. Dr. Begg, father of the late Dr. James Begg, published a treatise on the "Use of Organs," in which the following statement is attributed to the Rev. Alexander Hislop: "The Church of England has admitted into its articles this principle, that it belongs to 'the church' of her own authority, to 'decree rites and ceremonies.'

ple of the discretionary power of the church in regard to things not commanded by Christ in his Word, was the chief fountain from which flowed the gradually increasing tide of corruptions that swept the Latin church into apostasy from the gospel of God's grace. And as surely as causes produce their appropriate effects, and history repeats itself in obedience to that law, any Protestant church which embodies that principle in its creed is destined, sooner or later, to experience a similar fate. The same, too, may be affirmed of a church which formally rejects it and practically conforms to it. The reason is plain. The only bridle that checks the degenerating tendency of the church—a tendency manifested in all ages—is the Word of God: for the Spirit of grace Himself ordinarily operates only in connection with that Word. If this restraint be discarded, the downward lapse is sure. The words of the great theologian, John Owen—and the British Isles have produced no greater—are solemn and deserve to be seriously pondered: "The principle that the church hath power to institute any thing or ceremony belonging to

---

(Article 20) As a matter of historical fact, this principle was never agreed to by the Convocation that adopted the Thirty-nine Articles, this sentence being found neither in the first printed edition of the articles, nor in the draft of them that passed the Convocation, and which is still in existence, with the autograph signatures of the members; but it is believed to have been surreptitiously inserted by the hand of Queen Elizabeth herself, who had much of the over-bearing spirit of her father, Henry VIII., and who, as head of the church, which the English constitution made her, was determined to have a pompous worship under her ecclesiastical control." In support of this statement, reference is made to "authorities in *Presbyterian Review*, July, 1843." *The Use of Organs*, etc., by James Begg, D. D., (p. 150). See also Bannerman's *Church of Christ*, Vol. I., p. 339.

the worship of God, either as to matter or manner, beyond the observance of such circumstances as necessarily attend such ordinances as Christ himself hath instituted, lies at the bottom of all the horrible superstition and idolatry, of all the confusion, blood, persecution and wars that have for so long a season spread themselves over the face of the Christian world."

In view of such considerations as these, confirmed, as they are, by the facts of all past history, it is easy to see how irrelevant and baseless is the taunt flung by high churchmen, ritualists and latitudinarians of every stripe against the maintainers of the opposite principle, that they are narrow-minded bigots who take delight in insisting upon trivial details. The truth is exactly the other way. The principle upon which this cheap ridicule is cast is simple, broad, majestic. It affirms only the things that God has commanded, the institutions and ordinances that he has prescribed, and besides this, discharges only a negative office which sweeps away every trifling invention of man's meretricious fancy. It is not the supporters of this principle, but their opponents, who delight in insisting upon crossings, genuflexions and bowings to the east, upon vestments, altars and candles, upon organs and cornets, and "the dear antiphonies that so bewitch their prelates and their chapters with the goodly echo they make;" in fine, upon all that finical trumpery which, inherited from the woman clothed in scarlet, marks the trend backward to the Rubicon and the seven-hilled mart of souls.

But whatever others may think or do, Presbyterians cannot forsake this principle without the guilt of defection from their own venerable standards and from the testimonies sealed by the blood of their fathers. Among the principles that the Reformers extracted from the rubbish of corruption and held up to light again, none were more comprehensive, far-reaching and profoundly reforming than this. It struck at the root of every false doctrine and practice, and demanded the restoration of the true. Germany has been infinitely the worse because of Luther's failure to apply it to the full. Calvin enforced it more fully. The great French Protestant Church, with the exception of retaining a liturgical relic of popery, gave it a grand application, and France suffered an irreparable loss when she dragooned almost out of existence the body that maintained it. John Knox stamped it upon the heart of the Scottish Church, and it constituted the glory of the English Puritans. Alas! that it is passing into decadence in the Presbyterian churches of England, Scotland and America. What remains but that those who still see it, and cling to it as to something dearer than life itself, should continue to utter, however feebly, however inoperatively, their unchanging testimony to its truth? It is the acropolis of the church's liberties, the palladium of her purity. That gone, nothing will be left to hope, but to strain its gaze towards the dawn of the millennial day. Then—we are entitled to expect—a more thorough-going and glorious reformation will be effected than any that has blessed the church and the world since the magnificent propagation of Christianity by the labors of the inspired apostles themselves.

II.

Argument from the Old Testament.

In the Jewish dispensation God was pleased to proceed in accordance with the great principle which has been signalized, in regard to the introduction of instrumental music into the public worship of his people. He kept the ordering of this part of his formal and instituted worship in his own hands. There is positive proof that it was never made an element of that worship except by his express command. Without his warrant it was excluded; only with it was it employed.

1. Let us notice the operation of this principle with reference to *the tabernacle-worship*.

Moses received the mode of constructing the tabernacle and the order of its worship by divine revelation. "See, saith he, that thou make all things according to the pattern showed to thee in the mount." It will be admitted that the instructions thus divinely given descended to the most minute details—the sort of fabrics and skins to be used, and their diverse colors, the pins, the ouches and the taches, the ablutions, the vestments and the actions of the officiating priests and Levites, the ingredients of the holy ointment and the incense, the parts, the arrangements, the instruments of worship,—to everything connected with the tabernacle these specific directions referred. Of course, if God had intended instrumental music to be employed, it would have been included in these particular directions; the instruments would have been specified for its performance, and regulations enjoined for its use.

What, now, are the facts? No directions are given respecting instruments of music. Two instruments of sound are provided for, but they were of such a character as to make it impracticable to use them ordinarily as accompaniments of the voice in singing. The record is: "And the Lord spake unto Moses, saying, Make thee two trumpets of silver; of a whole piece shalt thou make them: that thou mayest use them for the calling of the assembly, and for the journeying of the camps." "And if ye go to war in your land against the enemy that oppresseth you, thou shalt blow an alarm with the trumpets; and ye shall be remembered before the Lord your God, and ye shall be saved from your enemies. Also in the days of your gladness, and in your solemn days, and in the beginnings of your months, ye shall blow with the trumpets over your burnt-offerings, and over the sacrifices of your peace-offerings; that they may be to you for a memorial before your God: I am the Lord your God." The blowing of these trumpets as a signal for marching, or for going to war, had certainly nothing to do with worship, neither did the call of the congregation to assemble belong to the performance of worship, any more than a church bell now, the ringing of which ceases when the services begin. There is nothing to show that the blowing of the trumpets, on festival days and at the beginning of months, over the offerings was accompanied by singing on the part of priests and Levites. There is no mention of that fact, and Jewish tradition opposes the supposition. Moreover, it is almost certain that the blowing of trumpets on such occasions was a representative act performed by the priests, and that consequently it was not accompanied by the singing of the congregation. It is true that there is one recorded exception (2 Chron. v. 12, 13) which occurred, however, when the tabernacle had given way to the temple. At the dedication of the latter edifice, the priests blew the trumpets at the same time that the Levites sang and played upon instruments of music, so as "to make one sound;" but it is evident that on that great occasion of rejoicing, what was aimed at was not musical harmony, but a powerful crash of jubilant sound. We are shut up to the conclusion that there was nothing in the tabernacle-worship, as ordered by Moses, which could be justly characterized as instrumental music.

This absence of instrumental music from the services of the tabernacle continued not only during the wanderings of the Israelites in the desert, but after their entrance into the promised land, throughout the protracted period of the Judges, the reign of Saul, and a part of David's. This is a noteworthy fact. Although David was a lover of instrumental music, and himself a performer upon the harp, it was not until some time after his reign had begun that this order of things was changed, and, as we shall see, changed by divine command. Let us hear the scriptural record (1 Chron. xxiii. 1-6): "So when David was old and full of days, he made Solomon his son king over Israel. And he gathered together all the princes of Israel, with the priests and the Levites. Now the Levites were numbered by the age of thirty years and upward: and their number by their polls, man by man, was thirty and eight thousand; of which twenty and four thousand were to set forward the work of the house of the Lord; and six thousand were officers and judges: moreover four thousand were porters; and four thousand praised the Lord with the instruments which I made, said David, to praise therewith. And David divided them into courses among the sons of Levi, namely, Gershon, Kohath and Merari." Now, how did David come to make this alteration in the Mosaic order which had been established by divine revelation? For the answer let us again consult the sacred record (1 Chron. xxviii. 11-13, 19): "Then David gave to Solomon his son the pattern of the porch, and of the houses thereof, and of the treasuries thereof, and of the inner parlors thereof, and of the place of the mercy-seat, and the pattern of all that he had by the Spirit, of the courts of the house of the Lord, and of all the chambers round about, of the treasuries of the house of God, and of the treasuries of the dedicated things: also for the courses of the priests and the Levites, and for all the work of the service of the house of the Lord, and for all the vessels of service in the house of the Lord. . . . All this, said David, the Lord made me understand in writing by his hand upon me, and all the works of this pattern." 2 Chron. xxix. 25, 26: "And he [Solomon] set the Levites in the house of the Lord with cymbals, with psalteries, and with harps, according to the commandment of David, and of Gad the king's seer, and of Nathan the prophet: for so was the commandment of the Lord by his prophets."

In the light of these statements of God's Word several things are made evident, which challenge our serious attention. First, instrumental music never was divinely warranted as an element in the tabernacle-worship until David received inspired instructions to introduce it, as preparatory to the transition which was about to be effected to the more elaborate ritual of the temple. Secondly, when the temple was to be built and its order of worship to be instituted, David received a divine revelation in regard to it, just as Moses had concerning the tabernacle with its ordinances. Thirdly, this direct revelation to David was enforced upon Solomon, and upon the priests and Levites, by inspired communications touching the same subject from the prophets Gad and Nathan. Fourthly, instrumental music would not have been constituted an element in the temple-worship, had not God expressly authorized it by his command. The public worship of the tabernacle, up to the time when it was to be merged into the temple, had been a stranger to it, and so great an innovation could have been accomplished only by divine authority. God's positive enactment grounded the propriety of the change.

Is it not clear that the great principle, that whatsoever is not commanded by God, either expressly or impliedly, in relation to the public worship of his house, is forbidden, meets here a conspicuous illustration? The bearing of all this upon the Christian church is as striking as it is obvious. If, under a dispensation dominantly characterized by external appointments, instrumental music could not be introduced into the worship of God's sanctuary, except in consequence of a warrant furnished by him, how can a church, existing under the far simpler and more spiritual dispensation of the gospel, venture, without such a warrant, to incorporate it into its public services? and that no such warrant can be pleaded will be made apparent as the argument expands.

2. Against the conclusiveness of this argument it is objected, that the Israelites were accustomed to use instrumental music at their option, and that especially was this the case on occasions of public rejoicing, when thanksgivings were, by masses of the people, rendered to God for signal benefits conferred by his delivering providence. So far as the allegation concerns the employment of that kind of music in private or social life, it is irrelevant to the scope of an argument which has reference explicitly and solely to its use in the public worship of God's house. This will rule out many of the instances which are cited to prove the untenableness of the principle contended for in this discussion.

There remains, however, another class of cases to which attention may be fairly directed, cases in which public worship appeared to be offered. Into this class fall the instances of Miriam's playing upon the timbrel at the Red Sea, the welcome of Saul and David by the women with singing, dancing and instrumental music, the like instance of Jephthah's daughter, the accompanying of the ark by David and Israel with bands of music, and the minstrelsy of the prophets to whom Saul joined himself. In reply to the objection based upon these instances, the general ground may be taken that they are examples not of church-worship, but of public rejoicing on the part of the nation or of communities, with the exception of the prophets' minstrelsy, which will be separately considered. Some special remarks are, however, pertinent in regard to them.

In the first place, it will be noticed from the account of the triumphant rejoicing on the shore of the Red Sea that the men sang only: "Then sang Moses and the children of Israel this song unto the Lord, and spake, saying," etc. What can be gathered from this simple singing of the males of Israel, in praise of God for their great deliverance, in favor of instrumental music in worship, it is rather difficult to see.

In the second place, it was Miriam and the women who used instruments of music on the occasion: "And Miriam the prophetess, the sister of Aaron, took a timbrel in her hand; and all the women went after her with timbrels and with dances." The argument of the objector proves too much. If from this instance the legitimacy of employing instrumental music in the public worship of the Jewish Church is to be inferred, so may the legitimacy of its use by women in that worship. But the history of the appointments of that worship furnishes no evidence of the tenableness of the latter inference. The contrary is proved. Women were excluded from any prominent, at least any official, function in the services of God's house in the Mosaic dispensation.[1] It was the males of Israel who were commanded to repair to Jerusalem on those festival occasions when bursts of instrumental music were united with the singing of praise in the temple-worship. Indeed, so far from the women taking an active part in

---

[1] The daughters of Heman, mentioned 1 Chron. xxv. 5, were not singers and performers on instruments in the public worship, for they are not included in the enumeration of the courses which follows.

that worship, it would seem to have been limited, as to its outward expression in sounds, to the priests and Levites, who, as the divinely appointed official representatives of the congregation, sang and played on instruments of music. The argument might do for a modern advocate of woman's rights, but it will hardly answer for the Jewish dispensation. It is as barren of results as was Miriam herself of issue.

In the third place, it again proves too much, if the word rendered "dances" is correctly translated. It would prove that religious dancing was an element in the prescribed worship of God's people. The consequence refutes the argument.

But to return to the general position, that the instances mentioned in the objection were those not of ecclesiastical worship, but of national rejoicing. Against this general view it is urged, in reply, that an unwarrantable distinction is made between the Jewish church and the Jewish nation. This raises the question whether such a distinction is valid. Were state and church identical? Did the members of the state act as members of the church? Did the members of the church act as members of the state? It may be admitted that, in the main—that is, with certain exceptions, such as the proselytes of righteousness, for example—the nation and the church were numerically coincident. Ordinarily—that is, with certain exceptions—the rite of circumcision designated one alike a member of the state and of the church. But that these two institutes were identical; that the functions of the one were the functions of the other, considered as organisms, is to my mind not susceptible of proof. It would be unsuitable here to enter at large into this question, but it lies across the track of the argument in hand, and a brief consideration of it, as it is not illogically interjected, will not be regarded as impertinent. The question is acutely and ably discussed by that great man, George Gillespie, in his *Aaron's Rod Blossoming*. I shall give a mere outline, the bare heads, of a part of his argument to prove that the Jewish state and church, although in the main the same materially, that is, as to personal constituents, were organically and formally distinct institutes; and I do this the more readily because Gillespie's valuable work is now rare and difficult of access. They are distinct:

(1.) In respect of laws. The judicial law was given to the state; the ceremonial law to the church.

(2.) In respect of acts. The members of the state did not, as such, worship God and offer sacrifices in the temple, etc.; and the members of the church did not, as such, inflict physical punishments.

(3.) In respect of controversies to be decided. Some concerned the Lord's matters, and were to be ecclesiastically settled; some the king's matters, and were to be civilly decided.

(4.) In respect of officers. The priests and Levites were church officers; magistrates and judges were state officers.

(5.) In respect of continuance. The Romans took away the Jewish state and civil government, but the Jewish church and ecclesiastical government remained.

(6.) In respect of variation. The constitution and government of the Jewish state underwent serious changes under different civil administrations; but we cannot say that the church was remodelled as often as the state was.

(7.) In respect of members. There were proselytes, the proselytes of righteousness, who were admitted to membership in the church with its privileges, but were not entitled to the privileges of members of the state.

(8.) In respect of government. In the prosecution of this argument to prove the distinctness of the Jewish church and state, Gillespie takes the ground that there were two Sanhedrims, one civil, the other ecclesiastical; and he cites, as maintaining that view, Zepperus, Junius, Piscator, Wolfius, Gerhard, Godwin, Bucerus, Walæus, Pelargus, Sopingius, the Dutch Annotators, Bertramus, Apollonius, Strigelius, the professors of Gröningen, Reynolds, Paget, L'Empereur, and Elias, cited by Buxtorf.

[This special argument Gillespie presses elaborately and acutely by more than a dozen separate considerations derived from Scripture. But as the question has been ably debated on both sides by men learned in Jewish affairs, no positive opinion is here expressed as to the conclusiveness of the proofs presented by the great Scotch divine.]

(9.) There was an ecclesiastical excommunication among the Jews different from the penalties inflicted by the criminal law of the state.

Such are the ribs merely of a powerful argument in favor of the distinction between the Jewish state and church, by one who had the reputation of being one of the astutest debaters in the Westminster Assembly of Divines. That distinguished scholar, Dr. Joseph Addison Alexander, expresses the opinion, in his *Primi-*

tive Church Offices, that the Jewish state and church were one organization, with two distinct classes of functions, one civil and another ecclesiastical. But Gillespie shows that the numerical components of some of the courts were different; they consisted of different men. Take either view, however, and the ends of this argument are met, more conclusively upon Gillespie's, it is true, but conclusively upon both. What the state as such did, the church as such did not do, and *vice versa*. And if this be so, it follows that the same thing holds in regard to the people. What they did in a national capacity they did not necessarily do in an ecclesiastical. When, then, Miriam and the women with her, the women who welcomed Saul and David returning home in triumph, the daughter of Jephthah celebrating her father's victory, and the mass of people who accompanied the ark in its transportation to Jerusalem, played on instruments of music, they were commemorating national events with appropriate national rejoicings. They were not acting worship as the church or as the members of the church.

In regard to the company of prophets whom Saul joined, it is sufficient to say that they were, in part, the poets and minstrels of the nation, and that as the incident occurred during the existence of the tabernacle, the incontestable proof which has been already exhibited, that instrumental music such as that which they employed was not allowed in its worship, is enough to sweep all ground from beneath the objection now considered against the operation of the great principle of limitation upon church worship for which I have contended. This holds good whether or not the view which has been presented as to these prophets be correct. Their playing on instruments had nothing to do with the public, formally instituted worship of the house of the Lord.

It has thus been shown, by a direct appeal to the Scriptures, that during all the protracted period in which the tabernacle was God's sanctuary the great principle was enforced, that only what God commands is permitted, and what he does not command is forbidden, in the public worship of his house. Moses with all his wisdom, the Judges with all their intrepidity, Saul with all his waywardness and self-will, David the sweet Psalmist of Israel with all his skill in the musical art, did not, any of them, venture to violate that principle, and introduce into the public services of God's house the devices of their imagination or the inventions of their taste. The lesson is certainly impressive, coming, as it does, from that distant age; and it behooves those who live in a dispensation this side of the cross of Calvary and the day of Pentecost to show cause, beyond a peradventure, why they are discharged from the duty of obedience to the divine will in this vitally important matter.

3. The next step in this argument is to show that no musical instruments were used in the synagogue-worship.

As this is almost universally admitted, no extended argument is needed to prove it. It might have been expected from the jealousy which God had always peculiarly manifested in enforcing the principle that without an express warrant from him nothing was to be introduced into the public worship of his people, and especially from the facts already emphasized that no instruments of music were allowed to be employed in the tabernacle, and that they were included in the service at the temple only in consequence of explicit divine instructions to that effect, it might have been expected that instrumental music would not have been incorporated into the worship of the Jews on ordinary Sabbath days not embraced in the three national festivals. This presumption is confirmed by the facts of the case.

The writers who have most carefully investigated Jewish antiquities, and have written learnedly and elaborately in regard to the synagogue, concur in showing that its worship was destitute of instrumental music. What singing there was, and there was not much of it in proportion to the other elements of worship, was plain and simple. In his great work *On the Ancient Synagogue*, Vitringa shows[1] that there were only two instruments of sound used in connection with the synagogue, and that these were employed, not in worship or along with it as an accompaniment, but as *publishing signals*—first, for proclaiming the new year; secondly for announcing the beginning of the Sabbath; thirdly, for publishing the sentence of excommunication; and fourthly, for heralding fasts. These were their sole uses. There were no sacrifices over which they were to be blown, as in the tabernacle and temple. And from the nature of the instruments it is plain that they could not have accompanied the voice in singing. They were only of two kinds—trumpets (*tubæ*), and rams'

---

[1] *De Synag. Vetere*, Lib. I., Pars i, Chap. 10. Lightfoot on Matt. vi. 2. See also Josephus, Ant. Jud., Lib. iii., Chap. 12.

horns or cornets (*buccinæ*). The former were straight, the latter curved. Nor is it to be supposed that the cornet, like the modern instrument of that name, was susceptible of modulation, and therefore of accompanying vocal melody. It had but one note, and was so easy to be blown that a child could sound it. Further, they were, for the most part, used not even in connection with the synagogue buildings, but were blown from the roofs of houses, so as to be heard at a distance. Enough has been said to prove that no instrumental music entered into the services of the Jewish synagogue.[1]

The elements of worship in the Mosaic dispensation were of two kinds:

(1.) The *generic* or *essential*. Those observed in the synagogue were the reading and exposition of God's Word, exhortation, prayers, accompanied with singing, if the common recitation by the people of parts of the Psalms can be so characterized, and the contribution of alms. Without here raising the question whether synagogues had an existence prior to the Babylonian exile, one would risk little in taking the ground that, during all the time of the church's development in the past, God's people had been accustomed to meet on Sabbath days for engagement in these essential parts of divine worship. The patriarchal dispensation being left out of account, in which, however, every sentiment of piety and reverence, the original institution of the seventh day as one of rest, and the acquaintance of the Israelites with the law of the Sabbath before the promulgation of the

---

[1] The orthodox Jews, even to the present day, oppose its use in the synagogue. The writer knew a congregation in Charleston, S. C., to be rent in twain in consequence of an attempt to introduce an organ.

Sinaitic law, render it highly probable that such a practice was maintained, a few reasons will be intimated in favor of its maintenance during the period of the Jewish economy:

First, The fourth commandment made the sacred observance of every Sabbath day obligatory. It is not reasonable to suppose that the law contemplated the merely individual and private keeping holy of the day.

Secondly, The Israelites, during their sojourn in the wilderness, were accustomed to worship every Sabbath day in mass at the tabernacle. It was accessible from every part of the encampment which was around it on every side. The proof of this is given in Lev. xxiii. 3: "Six days shall work be done: but the seventh day is the Sabbath of rest, an holy convocation." The prescriptive usage of meeting for worship on every Sabbath was thus established during their forty years' pilgrimage in the desert. In all that time during which they held weekly assemblies, let it also be observed, they knew nothing of instrumental music. It is altogether unreasonable to suppose that this habit, ingrained into them in the early period of their national existence and consecrated by innumerable sacred and splendid associations, would have ceased to be influential after their wanderings had ceased and they had been permanently located in the land of rest. Such an innovation upon their customs could only have occurred in consequence either of a divine command enforcing the change, or of a serious defection from their religious principles. We know that neither of these causes operated to produce the supposed revolution in their habits of worship. Upon their settlement in Canaan, they were of course dispersed in consequence of their tribal distribution throughout the length and breadth of the country from Dan to Beersheba, and, as the tabernacle was necessarily at any particular time confined to one spot, it was not accessible to congregations representing all Israel, except upon the occasions of the prescribed national festivals. What, then, were they doing on all the other Sabbaths of the year in their cities and towns, villages and rural neighborhoods? It cannot be supposed that on those Sabbaths they never met for worship.[1] This consideration is mightily enhanced by the fact that only the males of Israel were enjoined to attend the great annual festivals. Were the women, the mothers of Israel, the trainers of children and youth, left destitute of all public worship? The supposition cannot be entertained. Provision must have been made for their engagement in the stated public worship of their God.

Thirdly, The priests and Levites, when not occupied in the discharge of their formal, official duties at the temple, were distributed through the land, and there is evidence to show that they acted as teachers of schools. Is it likely that ministers of religion would have educated the people in everything but the divine law, or that they would have failed to assemble them on Sabbath days for the reception of religious instruction, or that such instruction would have been unattended by worship? It may be said that this amounts to no more than a presumption. But if so, it is a powerful pre-

---

[1] "Under every preceding dispensation the sanctity of the Sabbath had been a fundamental part of revealed religion; the synagogue worship goes back, possibly, to the captivity in Egypt, certainly to the captivity in Babylon."—Breckinridge's *Subjec. Theology*, p. 530.

sumption, and is strongly confirmed by other considerations, such as those that follow.

Fourthly, The Israelites were commanded to proclaim the incoming of the Sabbaths and the new moons by the blowing of trumpets. That these seasons were observed with the solemn worship of assemblies is rendered almost certain by the passage in 2 Kings, chapter iv., in which it is intimated that on those occasions the prophets were accustomed to hold meetings for instruction and worship. The Shunammite, whose son had been restored to life by Elisha, having lost the child by death, proposed to her husband to provide her with the necessaries for a journey to the prophet at Mount Carmel. His reply was, "Wherefore wilt thou go to him to-day? It is neither new moon, nor Sabbath?" The answer cannot be understood except upon the supposition here contended for—namely, that the Sabbaths and new moons were seasons of gathering for instruction and worship; and it is certain that Carmel was not Jerusalem, and that weekly Sabbaths and the beginnings of months did not occur only three times a year.

Fifthly, In Psalm lxxiv. 8, the Psalmist, in view of the devastation of the country by its enemies, thus laments: "They said in their hearts, Let us destroy them together: they have burned up all the synagogues of God in the land." It is not necessary to suppose that the buildings here rendered *synagogues* exactly corresponded with those erected for worship after the return from the Babylonish captivity, but they were places for worship.[1] Possibly they were, as Prideaux and others

---

[1] See Horne's *Introduction*, vol. ii. p. 102, for a confirmation of this view. It is there shown to have been advocated by Josephus and Philo, and also by Grotius, Ernesti, Whitby, Doddridge, and Lardner.

suggest, uncovered places of worship, *proseuchæ*, but they were buildings, else how could they have been burned? And that they were not the halls adjoining the temple, as some conjecture, is proved by the statement that they were throughout the land: "All the synagogues of God in the land." Were the temple buildings ubiquitous? In this exposition not a few eminent commentators agree. Dr. McCurdy, in Lange's Commentary on the place, says that these buildings were *places of meeting* in different parts of the land. Calvin remarks: "I readily take the Hebrew *moadim* in the sense of *synagogues*, because he says *all* the sanctuaries, and speaks expressly *of the whole land.*" Adam Clarke observes: "The word *moadey*, which we translate synagogues, may be taken in a more general sense, and mean any places where religious assemblies were held; and that such places and assemblies did exist long before the Babylonish captivity is pretty evident from different parts of Scripture."[1]

Dr. Plumptre, in the article on synagogues in Smith's *Dictionary of the Bible*, citing Vitringa *On the Synagogue* (pp. 271, ff.), says: "Jewish writers have claimed for their synagogues a very remote antiquity. In wellnigh every place where the phrase "before the Lord" appears they recognize in it a known sanctuary, a fixed place of meeting, and therefore a synagogue." This view is taken in the Targums of Onkelos and Jonathan.

---

[1] George Gillespie says: "After the tribes were settled in the land of promise synagogues were built in the case of an urgent necessity, because all Israel could not come every Sabbath day to the reading and expounding of the law in the place that God had chosen that his name might dwell there." *Eng. Pop. Cerem.* p. 116.

"On the one hand," says Dr. Plumptre, "it is probable that if new moons and Sabbaths were observed at all [it was shown above that they were], they must have been attended by some celebration apart from as well as at the tabernacle or the temple. . . On the other, so far as we find traces of such local worship, it seems to have fallen too readily into a fetich religion, sacrifices to ephods and teraphim, in groves and on high places, offering nothing but a contrast to the 'reasonable service,' the prayers, psalms, instruction in the law, of the later synagogue." This, to some extent not universally, is lamentably true; but the abuse proves the legitimate use of these stated seasons and places of public worship separately from the tabernacle and temple services.

The gatherings of the elders during the exile for instruction by the prophet, which are repeatedly mentioned in Ezekiel, infer that the practice of holding assemblies for worship and the hearing of the law antedated the captivity. The exiles carried the custom with them. The words in Ezek. xi. 15, 16, seem to imply that God manifested his gracious presence in these meetings of his people as in little sanctuaries, somewhat as in former and better times he had done at the greater sanctuaries in their native land. "This view is supported," remarks the learned author who has been quoted, "by the LXX., the Vulgate, and the Authorized Version. It is confirmed by the general *consensus* of Jewish interpreters."

If these arguments have availed to prove that the people of Israel were accustomed to hold stated meetings for worship apart from the services of the tabernacle and the temple, the well-ascertained practice of the post-exilian synagogues clearly establishes the absence of instrumental music from those weekly assemblies. For had that kind of music been employed in those meetings, it would inevitably have been continued in the synagogue-worship. Every conceivable consideration would have opposed its elimination—the powerful force of long-continued precedents, the prescriptive usages of the past hallowed by sacred associations, the conservative sentiment which resists a revolutionary innovation, and more than all the demands of human taste and the requirements of an acknowledged artistic standard. But it is certain that no instrumental music was used in the worship of the later synagogue. The argument is well-nigh irresistible.

If it be contended that instrumental music, which had previously existed, was purged out of the regular worship of the Jews by the post-exilian reformation, the question at issue is given up. For if the Jews reformed the worship of the church by abandoning instrumental music, much more should it have been discarded at the greater reformation inaugurated by Christianity. Otherwise it would be conceded that the Christian Church was less pure in its worship, less thoroughly reformed, than was the Jewish Church in its later and better state.

It has thus been shown that the essential parts of divine worship were maintained by the people of God in their ordinary Sabbath-day worship during the Jewish dispensation; and it is the purpose of this discussion, as it shall be developed, to evince the fact that only these essential elements of worship passed over into the Christian dispensation. They are permanent, and like the covenant of grace in its generic and essential features as contradistinguished to the specific and accidental, were designed to endure unchanged through all dispensations.

(2.) The second kind of elements of worship in the Mosaic economy was the *Specific* or *Accidental*, which was *Typical and Symbolical*, and as such temporary in its nature.[1] Warburton says that types and symbols are generically the same in that they are both representations, but they are specifically different in that the type represents something future, the symbol something past or present. Hence he regarded the sacraments of the New Testament as symbols. Thornwell observes that they differ from each other in the circumstance that types teach by analogy, and symbols by expressive signs. Without pausing to discuss the nature of the specific differences between them, or to consider the question whether some of the elements in the Jewish ritual service were not at the same time both typical and symbolical, I proceed to show that the types of the temple-worship did not, as is too often carelessly assumed, have exclusive reference to the sacrifice of Christ, but that some of them represented beforehand the effects to be produced in the New Testament dispensation by the Holy Ghost; and I will then attempt further to show, that the instrumental music of the

---

[1] Let it be observed that, in making this distinction between essential and accidental elements of worship, by the accidental are meant elements *divinely commanded*. With the Reformed and Puritan divines, I utterly repudiate the distinction as used by Prelatists to justify such accidental elements as human wisdom or church authority adds, without divine warrant, to the essential elements of worship.

temple-worship fell into the latter class, and therefore, as having fulfilled its typical and temporary office, passed away and vanished upon the introduction of the Christian economy. But before these points are developed, it is requisite that a few things be premised.

In the first place, no element in the synagogue-worship was typical and temporary. This is too evident to require argument. The reading and exposition of the divine Word, hortatory addresses, the singing of psalms, and the contribution of alms, are elements of worship which cannot be regarded as types foreshadowing substantial realities to come. They belong to the class essential and permanent.

In the second place, the essential and permanent elements of worship, as fundamental to all public religious service, entered of course into the temple-worship. In this respect there was no difference between the worship of the temple and that of the synagogue.

In the third place, whatever element of worship was absent from the synagogue and present in the temple was typical or symbolical in its character. Having in common what was essential and permanent, the specific difference between them lay in the possession by one of the accidental and temporary, and the non-possession by the other of the same. Now the only elements falling into this latter class were the typical and symbolical. These were embraced in the service of the temple and excluded from that of the synagogue. Consequently, as instrumental music was not included in the worship of the synagogue, but was in that of the temple, it must be regarded as having been either typical or symbolical. Symbolical it cannot be considered;

it must therefore have been typical. If so, the necessity is recognized of attempting, in the progress of this discussion, to show of what it was typical.

In the fourth place, some of the elements of the temple-service were directly and solely typical of Christ, especially as a priest and as the atoning sacrifice to be offered for sin. Others were typical only of the Holy Ghost; and still others were typical, at one and the same time, both of Christ and the Holy Spirit. To use the technically accurate language of theology, the impetration or acquisition of salvation is attributed to Christ, the application of it to the Holy Spirit. But the grace which applies the benefits secured by the work of Christ is closely related to the work by which they were acquired. Indeed it is itself acquired by the merit and intercession of the Redeemer. They therefore suppose and implicate each other. Consequently some of the types have a double reference to both. When they immediately represent the Holy Spirit they at the same time mediately represent Christ. Some of the positions taken in these preliminary remarks may be justly regarded and carried along with the discussion as assumptions demanding no proof, and others will be substantiated as the argument proceeds.

First, The offices and work of the Holy Spirit were as clearly and definitely predicted and promised in the Old Testament Scriptures as were those of Christ. The truth is that they cannot possibly be disjoined. Neither would be operative to salvation without the other. The whole Old Testament revelation, so far as it was evangelical, bore a twofold reference to the blood and the water, to the meritorious acquisition of salvation by the righteousness and atoning death of Christ and its efficacious application by the grace of the Holy Ghost. In the conception of redemption which we find everywhere in the Bible justification and sanctification are never dissociated. They are ever represented as the complementary and equally necessary factors of one whole and complete salvation. This is the very genius of the gospel as well before as after the death of the Son of God. As it was proclaimed to our first parents, revealed to Abel, Enoch and Noah, and, as the apostle expressly testifies, "preached before to Abraham," it was essentially promissory in its nature. The same promissory character was still more fully disclosed in the features of the Mosaic dispensation, in the Psalms and Prophets, and, as I hope to show, in the typical rites and ceremonies of the temple-service. That the person and offices of the Holy Spirit were distinctly known to believers under the old dispensation is proved by utterances in the Psalms, a book which represents the experience of God's true people in every condition of their history. In the 51st Psalm we have the prayers: "Take not thy Holy Spirit from me;" "Uphold me with thy free Spirit;" and in the 143rd, "Thy Spirit is good; lead me to the land of uprightness." Isaiah (chap. lxiii. 10) says: "They rebelled and vexed his Holy Spirit," which words, as they were spoken of the "house of Israel," suppose that they knew, or ought to have known, the Holy Spirit as their guide. It may be added that the sacred historians of the Old Testament over and over again assert, with reference to the heroic worthies of that dispensation, that the Spirit of the Lord came upon them. All this goes to show that the promises which related to the work of the Holy Spirit at a future period of the church's development were not unintelligible by those to whom they were delivered.

Let us cite some of those declarations which point to the work of the Spirit in the new dispensation. Isa. xxxii. 15-17: After describing the desolation that would be visited upon the land of Israel, the prophet says: "Until the Spirit be poured upon us from on high, and the wilderness be a fruitful field, and the fruitful field shall be counted for a forest. Then judgment shall dwell in the wilderness, and righteousness remain in the fruitful field. And the work of righteousness shall be peace; and the effect of righteousness quietness and assurance forever." Isa. xlii. 1: "Behold my servant, whom I uphold; mine elect, in whom my soul delighteth; I have put my Spirit upon him: he shall bring forth judgment to the Gentiles." Isa. xliv. 3, 4: "For I will pour water upon him that is thirsty, and floods upon the dry ground: I will pour my Spirit upon thy seed, and my blessing upon thine offspring; and they shall spring up as among the grass, as willows by the water courses." Isa. lix. 19, 20, 21: "So shall they fear the name of the Lord from the west, and his glory from the rising of the sun. When the enemy shall come in like a flood, the Spirit of the Lord shall lift up a standard against him. And the Redeemer shall come to Zion, and unto them that turn from transgression in Jacob, saith the Lord. As for me, this is my covenant with them, saith the Lord; my Spirit that is upon thee, and my words which I have put in thy mouth, shall not depart out of thy mouth, nor out of the mouth of thy seed, nor out of the mouth of thy seed's seed, saith the Lord, from henceforth and forever." This prophecy in regard to the Spirit resisting a flood of enemies is referred by the Rabbins to the coming of the Messiah. Ezek. xxxvi. 25–27: "Then will I sprinkle clean water upon you, and ye shall be clean: from all your filthiness, and from all your idols, will I cleanse you. A new heart also will I give you, and a new spirit will I put within you: and I will take away the stony heart out of your flesh, and I will give you an heart of flesh. And I will put my Spirit within you, and cause you to walk in my statutes, and ye shall keep my judgments and do them." Ezek. xxxvii. 13, 14: "And ye shall know that I am the Lord, when I have opened your graves, O my people, and brought you up out of your graves, and shall put my Spirit in you, and ye shall live, and I shall place you in your own land: then shall ye know that I the Lord have spoken it, and performed it, saith the Lord." Joel ii. 28, 29: "And it shall come to pass afterward, that I will pour out my Spirit upon all flesh; and your sons and your daughters shall prophesy, your old men shall dream dreams, your young men shall see visions: and also upon the servants and upon the handmaids in those days will I pour out my Spirit." For the reference of this glorious promise to New Testament times we have the inspired testimony of the apostle Peter on the day of Pentecost, when it was measurably but remarkably fulfilled. In close connection with the promise that a fountain shall be opened to the house of David, and to the inhabitants of Jerusalem, for sin and for uncleanness, Zechariah utters also the promise, xii. 10: "And I will pour upon the house of David, and upon the inhabitants of Jerusalem, the spirit of grace and of supplications." It matters little whether or not with some we take the word *spirit* here to indicate a disposition. That disposition can be produced only by the Holy Spirit. The apostle Paul, it deserves to be considered, terms the Spirit "that holy Spirit of promise," Eph. i. 13; and in Gal. iii. 13, 14, he speaks very explicitly about this matter: "Christ hath redeemed us from the curse of the law, being made a curse for us: for it is written, Cursed is every one that hangeth on a tree: that the blessing of Abraham might come on the Gentiles through Jesus Christ; that we might receive the promise of the Spirit through faith." How closely does he couple the atoning work of Christ and the applying work of the Spirit! And how clearly does he enounce the fact that the Spirit, as well as Christ, was promised in the ancient Scriptures and the early revelations made to the people of God!

Secondly, The offices of the Holy Ghost, together with their saving and joy-imparting effects, were typified, as well as the priestly work and expiatory death of Christ, in the services which were peculiar to the temple. In view of what has been shown concerning the clearness and fulness with which the work of the Spirit in New Testament times is announced in the prophetical writings we would be prepared to find this true upon an examination of the temple types; nor will we be disappointed by such an investigation. Those types, as well as the prophecies, proclaimed the gospel. They powerfully preached the whole salvation of the gospel,— the blood and the water, justification and sanctification. How could it be otherwise? As God intended by these typical elements to represent, as by object-lessons, the scheme of redemption to his ancient people who lived before its actual achievement, is it reasonable to suppose that he would have furnished an imperfect and inadequate pre-figuration of its essential parts? Would he have omitted all instruction beforehand in regard to the mode of its application? It is difficult to conceive how any theologian can fail to see the obvious foreshadowing in the temple furniture and service of the grace and work of the ever-blessed Spirit. I shall select for comment only those elements which appear with the greatest clearness to typify the offices of the Holy Spirit.

The Washing with Water. Why was water employed as a type, if not to signify what the New Testament Scriptures so unmistakably characterize under that figure? "Except a man," said the Lord Jesus, "be born of water and of the Spirit, he cannot enter into the kingdom of God." (Jno. iii. 5). The preposition here is omitted before the Spirit in the original, and the words may well be rendered "of water even the Spirit." At least this must be the meaning in the judgment of any one who would not co-ordinate external water with the almighty grace of the Holy Ghost in the new creation of the soul. And to talk of one's being spiritually born in part of an outward symbol is to speak unintelligibly. Paul several times uses washing and water to signify cleansing by the Holy Spirit. Eph. v. 26: "That he might sanctify and cleanse it [the church] with the washing of water by the word." 1 Cor. vi. 11: "And such were some of you; but ye are washed, but ye are sanctified, but ye are justified in the name of the Lord Jesus, and by the Spirit of our God." Tit. iii. 5: "According to his mercy he saved us, by the washing of regeneration and [or, even the] renewing of the Holy Ghost." John emphasizes the issue of water and blood from the side of Jesus on the cross, and declares, "This is he that came by water and blood, even Jesus Christ; not by water only, but by water and blood. And it is the Spirit that beareth witness, because the Spirit is truth. And there are three that bear witness in earth, the Spirit, and the water, and the blood; and these three agree in one." (Jno. xx. 34; 1 Jno. v. 6, 8.) The Spirit bears witness both to justification and sanctification. It is he who sanctifies and he who bears witness with his own work in the soul. The analogy, then, between the type and the anti-type, as to the offices respectively discharged, leads to the conclusion that the lavers and ablutions of the temple typified the grace of the Holy Spirit. This view is far from being singular. It has the support of the illustrious Lightfoot. "The end of it [the laver] was," he says, "to wash the hands and feet of the priests; but the most ultimate end was to signify the washing and purifying by the Spirit of grace, which is so oft called *water* in the Scripture. And so the sprinkling of the blood of the sacrifice, and the washing in the water of the laver, did read the two great divinity lectures, of washing by the blood of Christ from guilt, and by the grace of God from filthiness and pollution."[1] This witness is true, and his learning and piety render

---

[1] *Works*, Vol. ix., p. 419; London, 1823. Fairbairn takes substantially the same view: *Typology of Scripture*, Vol. ii., pp. 212, 213. See also M'Ewen, *Types*, Bk. iii., § 3.

it superfluous to cite the testimony of others to the same purpose.

The Anointing Oil. Is it not clear from Scripture that this typified the Holy Spirit? Under the Old Testament economy priests, prophets and kings were anointed. Did the anointing oil of the temple signify that Christ would anoint himself? or rather, did it not prefigure his anointing by the Holy Ghost? He is the Christ, God's anointed One, and the holy Unction was the Spirit of wisdom, power and grace. Acts x. 38: "How God anointed Jesus of Nazareth with the Holy Ghost and with power." This direct testimony is sufficient. The anointing oil of the temple discharged the typical office of prefiguring the holy Unction with which Jesus was anointed, and who, coming from him upon all his people, teacheth them all things. (1 Jno. ii. 27.) This view also is sustained by the authority of the distinguished scholar who has already been cited. "The oil and anointing," he observes, "wherewith the priests and the vessels of the Lord's house were sanctified, did denote the Word and the Spirit of God, whereby he sanctifieth the vessels of his election, even persons of his choice, to his service and acceptance."[1]

The Oil in the Golden Candlestick. Taking into view the analogy of Scripture teaching, one cannot doubt that this oil typified the Holy Spirit. I cite the remarks upon this point of the Rev. Patrick Fairbairn, in his *Typology of Scripture:*[2] "This symbol has received such repeated illustration in other parts of Scripture,

---

[1] *Ibid.*, p. 440. This view is also maintained by M'Ewen, *Types*, Bk. iii. § 3.

[2] Vol. ii., pp. 257, 258.

that there is scarcely any room for difference of opinion as to its fundamental import and main idea. In the first chapter of Revelation, the image occurs in its original form, 'the seven golden lamps' (not candlesticks, as in our version, but the seven lamps on the one candlestick) are explained to mean 'the seven churches.' These churches, however, not as of themselves, but as replenished by the Spirit of God, and full of holy light and energy; and hence in the fourth chapter of the same book we again meet with seven lamps of fire before the throne of God, which are said to be 'the seven Spirits of God'—either the one Spirit of God in his varieties of holy and spiritual working,[1] or seven presiding spirits of light fitted by that Spirit for the ministrations referred to in the heavenly vision. Throughout Scripture, as we have already seen in chapter three of this part, oil is uniformly taken for a symbol of the Holy Spirit. It is so, not less with respect to its light-giving property, as to its qualities for anointing and refreshment; and hence the prophet Zechariah (chap. iv.) represents the exercise of the Spirit's gracious and victorious energy in behalf of the church under the image of two olive trees pouring oil into the golden candlestick, the church being manifestly imaged in the candlestick, and the Spirit's assisting grace in the perpetual current of oil with which it was supplied."[2]

---

[1] This is probably the true view.

[2] In opposition to Fairbairn, and in agreement with the majority of orthodox commentators, I would regard the golden candlestick as itself a type of Christ, and the *lights* merely, the *lamps* of revelation, as representing the Church. The oil, with Fairbairn, I take to typify the illuminating grace of the Holy Ghost; but the true Container of that oil

The Feast of Pentecost. "This festival," says Horne, in his Introduction,[1] "had a typical reference to the miraculous effusion of the Holy Spirit upon the apostles and first-fruits of the Christian Church on the day of Pentecost, . . on the fiftieth day after the resurrection of Jesus Christ." He refers, in support of this view, to Schultz, Lamy, Lightfoot, Michaelis, Reland and Alber.

Horne further says:[2] "One of the most remarkable ceremonies performed at this feast, in the later period of the Jewish polity, was the libation or pouring out of water, drawn from the fountain or pool of Siloam, upon the altar. As, according to the Jews themselves,[3] this water was an emblem of the Holy Spirit, Jesus Christ applied the ceremony and the intention of it to himself when he cried, saying, If any man thirst, let him come unto me and drink. (Jno. vii. 37–39.)"

Treating of this feast, Fairbairn makes the following instructive remarks:[4] "The rite that commemorated the typical redemption had to take precedence of anything belonging to the coming harvest, even of the presentation of its first ripening sheaf. But the work of redemption being finished, and the feast of fat things so

---

is originally Christ himself, not the church (except, perhaps, derivatively), which receives it from him and manifests it in a world of darkness. See M'Ewen, *Types*, Bk. iii., § 3.

[1] Vol. ii., p. 126.

[2] *Ibid.*, p. 127. M'Ewen strongly urges this typical significance of the Feast of Pentecost.

[3] In confirmation of this assertion the author quotes the following passage from the Jerusalem Talmud: "Why is it called the place or house of drawing? Because from thence they draw the Holy Spirit: as it is written, And ye shall draw water with joy from the wells of salvation."

[4] *Typol. Scrip.*, Vol. ii. p. 311.

long in preparation being ready, then the freest welcome is given to come and be satisfied with the loving-kindness of the Lord. And Christ having suffered and been glorified, what day could be so fitly chosen for the descent of the Holy Ghost as the day of Pentecost? For to what end was the Spirit given? To take of the things of Christ, and show them to Christ's people; that is, to turn the riches of his purchased redemption from being a treasure laid up among the precious things of God, into a treasure received and possessed by his people, so that they might be able to rejoice, and call others to rejoice with them, in the goodness of his house. Now the work of God is finished, henceforth the fruitful experience of it among his people proceeds; and the first-fruits of the Spirit having assuredly been given, he can never withdraw his hand till the whole inheritance of blessing is enjoyed."

Instrumental Music.

In the first place, it has already been shown that neither by God's direction nor in the actual practice of his people in the old dispensation were instruments of music, susceptible of modulation, employed elsewhere in public worship than in the temple. They were not used in the tabernacle until David was preparing to build the temple, or in the synagogue.

In the second place, it has also been shown that whatever element of worship was embraced in the temple-service, and was absent from that of the synagogue, was typical in its character. This was true of instrumental music. Therefore, as an element of the temple-worship, it was typical.

In the third place, it has been proved that some of the elements contained in the temple-service were typical of the Holy Spirit and of the effects to be produced by him in the New Testament dispensation, such as consecration, illumination, purification, and the conversion of souls; and now,

In the fourth place, I lay down the proposition that the instrumental music of the temple-worship was typical of the joy and triumph of God's believing people to result from the plentiful effusion of the Holy Ghost in New Testament times.

It was suited to discharge such a significant office in the age in which God saw fit to prescribe its employment as a part of a typical ritual. It produces an exhilaration of the senses, and that is about all that it does produce. We have seen that the Israelites, like all other peoples, employed it in their national and secular rejoicings. Now, the Mosaic dispensation was not peculiarly a dispensation of the Spirit. It is a distinctive glory of the Christian economy that it is "the ministration of the Spirit." "But," says Paul, "we speak the wisdom of God in a mystery, even the hidden wisdom, which God ordained before the world unto our glory: which none of the princes of this world knew: for had they known it, they would not have crucified the Lord of glory. But as it is written, Eye hath not seen, nor ear heard, neither have entered into the heart of man, the things which God hath prepared for them that love him. But God hath revealed them unto us by his Spirit: for the Spirit searcheth all things, yea, the deep things of God." 1 Cor. ii. 7–10. This revelation, partially made in the old dispensation, is far more fully unfolded even in this life in the present, and will be still more amply and gloriously in the heavenly. "But if," also says the same apostle, "the ministration of death, written and engraven in stones, was glorious, so that the children of Israel could not steadfastly behold the face of Moses for the glory of his countenance; which glory was to be done away: how shall not the ministration of the Spirit be rather glorious? For if the ministration of condemnation be glory, much more doth the ministration of righteousness exceed in glory. For even that which was made glorious had no glory in this respect, by reason of the glory that excelleth." (2 Cor. iii. 7-10.) In the New Testament we are clearly taught the reason of this. It was not meet that the Holy Spirit should be copiously poured out before the actual offering up of the great atoning sacrifice and the entrance of the true high priest into the heavenly holy of holies. "In the last day, that great day of the feast, Jesus stood and cried, saying, If any man thirst, let him come unto me, and drink. He that believeth on me, as the Scripture hath said, out of his belly shall flow rivers of living water. (But this spake he of the Spirit, which they that believe on him should receive; for the Holy Ghost was not yet given, because that Jesus was not yet glorified.") (Jno. vii. 37-39.) As, then, in the ancient dispensation, the veil of the temple was not rent in twain, as the full liberty of adoption and boldness of access into the presence of God, with the assurance of faith and hope, which makes heaven begin on earth, were not granted to the worshipper, it pleased God to typify the spiritual joy to spring from a richer possession of the Holy Spirit through the sensuous rapture engendered by the passionate melody of stringed instruments and the clash of cymbals, by the blare of trumpets and the ringing of harps. It was the instruction of his children in a lower school, preparing them for a higher. Meanwhile, it must not be forgotten, they were habitually recalled, even in that dispensation, by the simpler and more spiritual worship of their weekly assemblies, to a service of God which, as it had always existed in the past, contained in itself a prophecy of permanence through the whole future development of the church.

That the instrumental music of the temple, which, as we have seen, was introduced into its services only by express divine warrant, was typical, and therefore temporary, is further proved by the fact that it was not practised in the apostolic church. This, it is true, remains to be established in the progress of the argument, but it is so generally admitted that it may here be assumed. Most certainly if the King and Law-giver of the church had intended that kind of music to accompany its singing of praise under the New Testament, he would have instructed its inspired organizers to that effect. That they did not sanction it is evidence that he did not command it, and that in turn proves that it was designed to be merely typical during the continuance of the temple-worship.

Now, it must have been typical, either of Christ in his person or offices, or of the use of instrumental music by the church in the New Testament dispensation or some other outward action, or of the Holy Spirit in his person or offices, or of an effect produced by his grace. There is no other supposition I can think of. There is no conceivable sense in which it could have typified the person or offices of Christ. There is no sense in which it is supposable that it typified any other external action of the church than the use of instrumental music. It could not have typified the use of instrumental music itself, for that would involve the absurdity of a thing typifying itself—of an identity of the representation with the thing represented, of a type with its antitype. We cannot imagine any way in which it could have typified either the invisible person or the offices of the Holy Ghost. We are shut up, then, to the position that it was typical of an effect to be produced by the grace of the divine Spirit; and I but echo the opinion of eminent and godly divines in maintaining that it was designed to be a type of that spiritual and triumphant joy which is engendered by the plentiful effusion of the Holy Ghost upon believers under the Christian dispensation. The Spirit having been poured out, and that abundant joy of believers having been experienced, the shadow gave way to the substance, the type to the antitype.

In order to evince the fact that this view is not novel or singular, I adduce the testimony of a few distinguished theologians, showing, in general, that instrumental music was typical, and, in particular, that it was typical of the graces of the Holy Spirit.

"To sing the praises of God upon the harp and psaltery," says Calvin, "unquestionably formed a part of the training of the law and of the service of God under that dispensation of *shadows and figures;* but they are not now to be used in public thanksgiving."[1] He

---

[1] On Ps. lxxi. 22.

says again: "With respect to the *tabret, harp, and psaltery,* we have formerly observed, and will find it necessary afterwards to repeat the same remark, that the Levites, under the law, were justified in making use of instrumental music in the worship of God; it having been his will to train his people, while they were yet tender and like children, by such rudiments until the coming of Christ. But now, when the clear light of the gospel has dissipated the *shadows* of the law and taught us that God is to be served in a simpler form, it would be to act a foolish and mistaken part to imitate that which the prophet enjoined only upon those of his own time."[1] He further observes: "We are to remember that the worship of God was never understood to consist in such outward services, which were only necessary to help forward a people as yet weak and rude in knowledge in the spiritual worship of God. A difference is to be observed in this respect between his people under the Old and under the New Testament; for now that Christ has appeared, and the church has reached full age, it were only to bury the light of the gospel should we introduce the *shadows* of a departed dispensation. From this it appears that the Papists, as I shall have occasion to show elsewhere, in employing instrumental music cannot be said so much to imitate the practice of God's ancient people as to ape it in a senseless and absurd manner, exhibiting a silly delight in that worship of the Old Testament which was *figurative,* and terminated with the gospel."[2]

"The first question," says Ames (Amesius) in his *Church Ceremonies,*[3] "was, If the primitive church had

---

[1] On Ps. lxxxi. 3.   [2] On Ps. xcii. 1.   [3] P. 404.

such chaunting idol-service, as is in our cathedral churches. The Rejoinder [Dr. Burgess] after some words spent about singing (about which he bringeth not the least resemblance of that in question, until the fourth age [century] after Christ) excepteth first, That organall music was God's ordinance in the Old Testament, and that not significant, or typicall; and therefore is sinfully called idol service. . . . To this I say (1), That his denying of organall music to have been *significant or typicall* is without reason, and against the current of our divines [N. B.]; taken, as it may seeme, out of Bellarmine (*On the Mass*, B. 2, C. 15), who useth this evasion against those words of P. Martyr: 'Musicall organs perteyne to the Jewish ceremonie, and agree no more to us than circumcision.' So that we may neglect it, and take him as saying, that nothing which was ordained in the Old Testament (no, not sacrificing of beasts) is now an idol-service."

Yet, Bellarmin, who is here referred to by Ames as evading the judgment of Peter Martyr, himself expresses the same judgment in another place.[1] "Justinus," he observes, "saith that the use of instruments was granted to the Jews for their imperfection, and that therefore such instruments have no place in the church. We [Bellarmin and the Catholics] confess indeed that the use of musical instruments agreeth not alike with the perfect and with the imperfect, and that therefore they began but of late to be admitted into the church." Bellarmin lived from 1542 to 1621.

---

[1] *De Bon. Operibus, Lib.* i. *Cap.* 17. We appeal from Philip drunk to Philip sober—from Bellarmin the partisan to Bellarmin the theologian.

This last mentioned opinion of the great polemic Cardinal had been previously expressed by Thomas Aquinas, the angelic doctor of the Church of Rome, in his *Summa Theologica*.[1] "Instruments of music," he says, "such as harps and psalteries, the church does not adopt for divine praises, lest it should seem to Judaize." "Instruments of this sort more move the mind to delight, than form internally a good disposition. Under the Old Testament, however, there was some utility in such instruments, both because the people were more hard and carnal, and needed to be stirred up by instruments of this kind as by promises of earthly good, and also because material instruments of this sort *figured* something."

"It is evident," says Zwingle,[2] "that that same ecclesiastical chanting and roaring in our temples (scarce also understood of the priests themselves) is a most foolish and vain abuse, and a most pernicious let to piety. In the solemn worship of God, I do not judge it more suitable than if we should recall the incense, tapers and other *shadows of the law* into use. I say again, to go beyond what we are taught is most wicked pervicacity."

Voetius, in his great work, the *Ecclesiastical Polity*, elaborately argues against the use of instrumental music in the Christian church, and among the arguments which he advances employs this: "Because it savors of Judaism, or a worship suited to a childish condition under the Old Testament economy; and there might with equal justice be introduced into the churches of

---

[1] II. ii. 2, xci., A. ii., 4, *et conclusio: Tom.* iv., *Ratisbonæ*, 1884, p. 646.
[2] *Act. Disp.* ii. p. 106, quoted by Ames.

the New Testament the bells of Aaron, the silver trumpets of the priests, the horns of the Jubilee, harps, psalteries and cymbals, with Levitical singers, and so the whole cultus of that economy, or the beggarly elements of the world, according to the words of the apostle in the fourth chapter of Galatians."[1]

Suicer, in his *Thesaurus*,[2] argues at length to vindicate Clement of Alexandria from the representation that he favored the use of instruments in the church, and to show that he and Isidore of Pelusium regarded the instrumental music of the Old Testament as typical of the joyful praise of the New Testament church for the rich benefits of an accomplished redemption. He cites a canon of one of the Councils of Carthage to this effect: "On the Lord's day let all instruments of music be silenced;" and remarks that but few in his own time favored the use of instruments in the church.

George Gillespie, in his *Assertion of the Government of the Church of Scotland*,[3] says: "The Jewish Church, not as it was a church but as it was Jewish, had an High Priest, typifying our great High Priest, Jesus Christ. As it was Jewish, it had musicians to play upon harps, psalteries, cymbals and other musical instruments in the temple."

David Calderwood, the author of the celebrated work, *Altare Damascenum* (*Altar of Damascus*) and of a valuable History of the Church of Scotland, says in his book, *The Pastor and the Prelate*:[4] "The Pastor

---

[1] Lib. ii., Tract. ii., Cap. iii., Tom. i., Amstel., p. 554.
[2] On word, *Organ*.
[3] Ch. iii., p. 13: *The Presbyterian's Armory*, Vol. i.
[4] P. 4, *Presbyterian's Armory*, Vol. iii.

loveth no music in the house of God but such as edifieth, and stoppeth his ears at instrumental music, as serving for the pedagogy of the untoward Jews under the law, and being *figurative* of that spiritual joy whereunto our hearts should be opened under the gospel. The *Prelate* loveth carnal and curious singing to the ear, more than the spiritual melody of the gospel, and therefore would have antiphony and organs in the cathedral kirks, upon no greater reason than other *shadows* of the law of Moses; or lesser instruments, as lutes, citherns and pipes might be [to be] used in other kirks."

"As good an argument," remarks Dr. James Begg, "can be made for the use of incense, priests, sacrifices, indeed of the whole temple system, as for the use of instrumental music in Christian worship."[1]

Dr. Killen, in his *Ancient Church*, says:[2] "As the sacrifices, offerings and other observances of the temple, as well as the priests, the vestments, and even the building itself, had an emblematic meaning, it would appear that the singing, intermingled with the music of various instruments of sound, was also typical and ceremonial."

In a striking argument against the use of instrumental music in the worship of the Christian church, the Rev. Dr. Alexander Blaikie, an American minister, says:[3] "These [musical instruments] continued in the temple-service of Jehovah so long as 'the first tabernacle was yet standing,' and no longer; for so soon as

---

[1] On *the Use of Organs*, etc., p. 18. [2] P. 216.
[3] *The Organ and other Musical Instruments, as noted in the Holy Scriptures.*

the way into the holiest of all was made manifest (Heb. ix. 8,) the bondage (beloved by every Jew) of these 'weak and beggarly elements' was in the worship of God forever done away. He, 'in whom dwelleth all the fulness of the Godhead bodily,' took the whole 'hand-writing of ordinances out of the way, nailing it to his Cross.' Instruments of music in the worship of God had there fulfilled their mission, in common with the blood of bulls, of goats, and the ashes of heifers, and they finished their course when Jesus died. No blast of 'rams'-horns,' nor other 'things without life-giving sound' had any longer a place with acceptance in the worship of Jehovah. The ceremonial, sensual, and ritual in his worship there forever ceased to be appointed by and acceptable to God, when he who 'spake as never man spake' exclaimed, 'It is finished.'"

In his reply to the statement of the Rev. Dr. Ritchie, submitted to the Presbytery of Glasgow in favor of the introduction of an organ in St. Andrew's church, Glasgow (the case was decided in May, 1808, adversely to Dr. Ritchie), the Rev. Dr. Porteous remarks: "It seems to be acknowledged by all descriptions of Christians, that among the Hebrews instrumental music in the public worship of God was essentially connected with sacrifice—with the morning and evening sacrifice, and with the sacrifices to be offered up on great and solemn days. But as all the sacrifices of the Hebrews were completely abolished by the death of our blessed Redeemer, so instrumental music . . . being so intimately connected with sacrifice, and belonging to a service which was ceremonial and typical, must be abolished with that service; and we can have no warrant to recall it into the Christian church, any more than we have to use other abrogated rites of the Jewish religion, of which it is a part."¹

That able and judicious theologian, Dr. Ridgley, speaks very expressly, not only of the typical nature of the instrumental music employed in the temple, but of that which it was designed to typify. He says: "It may be observed, that how much soever the use of musical instruments which were in this worship may be concluded to be particularly adapted to that dispensation, as they were typical of that spiritual joy which the gospel church should obtain by Christ; yet the ordinance of singing remains a duty, as founded on the moral law."²

To the objection that "those arguments that have been taken from the practice of the Old Testament church to prove singing an ordinance may, with equal justice, be alleged to prove the use of instrumental music," he replies: "Though we often read of music being used in singing the praises of God under the Old Testament, yet if what has been said concerning its being a type of that spiritual joy which attends our praising God for the privilege of that redemption which Christ has purchased be true, then this objection will

---

¹ Dr. Candlish, *The Organ Question*, pp. 87, 88. It may be said in answer, that on the same ground singing ought to be abolished. But, first, singing was not as peculiarly connected with sacrifice as was the blowing of trumpets; secondly, that the use of instruments was peculiar to the temple service, whereas singing was not. The argument only holds in regard to the specific and temporary elements of worship, not to the generic and permanent.

² *Body of Divinity*, Quest. CLIV., Vol. iv., p. 82, Philadelphia, 1815.

appear to have no weight, since this type is abolished together with the ceremonial law."[1]

I have heard the view maintained that the reason why this music was not in use in the synagogue worship was that it would have involved a violation of the law commanding the Sabbath day to be kept holy; that it required a species of labor which, as it was not necessary, would have violated the commandment enjoining abstinence from all unnecessary work on that day. And in support of this view, it is claimed that instrumental music was permitted, and was actually employed on the week-days between the Sabbaths. In reply I would say:

In the first place, the allegation, that instrumental music was used on week-days in the synagogue before the Christian dispensation began, needs to be confirmed. The fact that such a practice now exists, or has existed for a long time, proves nothing. The rationalism and indifferentism of many of the modern Jews would be sufficient to account for the fact, just as that heterodox temper affords an explanation of the employment of organs in the synagogue-worship even on the Sabbath.

In the second place, if the allegation were true, it would establish nothing in opposition to the view maintained in this discussion. For, during the Mosaic dispensation, the Jews ever manifested a tendency to disobey divine commands and contemn divine ordinances, in the assertion of their own will and the gratification of their own taste—a disposition which frequently incited them to flagrantly idolatrous worship.

---

[1] *Ibid.*, pp. 87, 88.

And although, after the Babylonian captivity open idolatry ceased, the same disposition continued, and called forth the rebuke administered by Christ to the Scribes and Pharisees for making void the commandments of God by human traditions. The oral law overlay the written, tradition superseded the Bible.

Furthermore, it may be questioned, whether this reputed worship of small numbers of persons in a synagogue on the days of the week could be put into the category of solemn, formal, public worship, such as that which obtained on Sabbath days.

In the third place, it is admitted that instrumental music was not employed in the synagogue on the Sabbath. The reason assigned is, that it would have infringed the law of the Sabbath requiring a cessation of all unnecessary work. Now, the question arises, how, in view of that law, it was employed in the temple on the Sabbath? The answer given is, that God, in that case, by his authority relaxed the rigor of the fourth commandment, and warranted work which otherwise would have been unjustifiable. I rejoin:

A relaxation of the Sabbatic law, in favor of the temple-services, is not granted. Whatever was necessary or proper, according to God's appointment, in order to the observance of his worship, was provided for in that law. It was not requisite for God to dispense with his own authority to secure compliance with it.

Further, if, according to the supposition, God relaxed his law in one case, the question is, Why did he not relax it in the other? If for the temple, why not for the synagogue? The same authority was sufficient for the relaxation in the latter case as well as in the former.

But this hypothesis of a relaxation of the law being discharged, the question returns, Why was not instrumental music employed on the Sabbath in the synagogue as well as in the temple? The answer is, Because God did not so command. He commanded it to be used in the temple; he did not, as he might have done, command it to be used in the synagogue. Now, why? There must be an adequate reason for the difference. What was it? The only reply which appears to furnish a solution of the difficulty is, that the temple-worship was typical, that of the synagogue not. The employment of types in the synagogue would have contradicted the very idea of the temple. The reason of the singular and exceptional existence of the latter was that it embraced a typical service. To have made the types common would therefore have subverted the temple.

The argument may be made still clearer by testing it upon the instance of sacrifices. They were offered at the temple on the Sabbath. Why were they not offered in the synagogue on that day? Will the Jew himself contend that the reason was that the law of the Sabbath would have been violated? He himself will concede that sacrifices, as typical, could only have been offered at the temple. If he deny, he denies the meaning of sacrifices and the genius of the Jewish religion. So was it with all the types, including instrumental music. Would he say that sacrifices were permissible in the synagogue on other than Sabbath days? Would he say that such a practice ever actually obtained? He must find, then, another reason why sacrifices were not offered in the synagogue on the Sabbath, than the infraction of the Sabbatic law which they would have involved. The same argument holds good in relation to instrumental music. But the question here is with the Jew, and the attempt to convince him, without the concurrence of almighty grace, would be as operative as an effort to reduce Gibraltar with an argument.

It has been proved by this special line of argument that, in consequence of the absence of a divine command justifying its use, instrumental music was not included in the synagogue-worship; that, as Christ, the procurer of redemption, was promised, so also the Holy Spirit, the applier of redemption, was promised, in the Old Testament—that a whole salvation by blood and by water was revealed in its didactic statements, its prophecies, and its types; that the elements in the temple service, which were not embraced in that of the synagogue, were typical; that some of these were typical of the Holy Ghost and the effects to be produced by his grace in New Testament times; and that among them instrumental music must be classed. From all this it follows, first, that to bring over into the new dispensation the features of worship which belonged to the temple, and not to the synagogue, is more unwarrantable in us than the importation of the distinctive elements of the temple-worship into the synagogue would have been to the Jews; secondly, that, as the types of the Holy Spirit in the temple-service are fulfilled in his application to believers of the benefits of a purchased redemption, to retain them in the Christian church is as much to dishonor him as to retain bloody sacrifices would dishonor Christ; and thirdly, that therefore, as instrumental music in the temple-worship was one of those types, its employment in the public services of the Christian church is at once unwarrantable and dishonoring to the ever-blessed Spirit.

4. To all this argument derived from the Old Testament it is triumphantly objected that the Psalms exhort all men to praise God with instruments of music, and that they were designed to be sung in every age of the church. The objection is as futile as it is popular.

In the first place, why did not David, who was one of the principal authors of the Psalms, introduce at an earlier period than he did instrumental music into the tabernacle worship? The reply is, that he was not divinely commanded to do it. Why did not Moses, who was an accomplished psalmist, and who heard the thrilling sound of timbrels in the great rejoicing over the discomfited host of Pharaoh on the shore of the Red Sea, incorporate this kind of music as an accompaniment of singing into that worship? The answer is, Because he had no divine warrant for such a measure. We have seen that David, by divine command, prepared instruments of music, and directed them to be used in the temple when that edifice should be erected. He would have had no right to take that step had he not been inspired and commanded to do so by God, who alone possessed the prerogative to dictate the mode in which he should be worshipped. It deserves inquiry, too, whether any of the Psalms which are ascribed to David, in which musical instruments are mentioned, have any reference to their employment in the public worship of God's house. Let those who are wont to plead the authority of his name examine the 57th, 108th, and 144th Psalms, and discover in them, if they can, anything more than references to his individual worship. The 81st is attributed to Asaph, and may well have been composed after the dedication of the temple.

It may also be observed, while this Psalm is under notice, that the argument derived from it in favor of the early use of musical instruments by the Israelites has no value. The words are: "Take a psalm, and bring hither the timbrel, the pleasant harp with the psaltery. Blow up the trumpet in the new moon, in the time appointed, on our solemn feast day. For this was a statute for Israel, and a law of the God of Jacob. This he ordained in Joseph for a testimony, when he went out through the land of Egypt." The statute, law, ordinance here mentioned manifestly relates especially to the feast of the Passover, which, when it occurred at the new moon, was attended with the solemn blowing of trumpets, as the parallel passage shows: Ex. xiii. 8, 9, 14-16. If this is not deemed satisfactory, let the statute, law or ordinance be pointed out which enforced the use of timbrels, harps and psalteries upon the Israelites in connection with their exodus from Egypt. Until that is done loose assertion will avail nothing.

The ninety-second Psalm is anonymous, and refers to individual worship. The thirty-third, which is anonymous, does not necessarily relate to public worship. The ninety-eighth, one hundred and forty-ninth and one hundred and fiftieth are also anonymous, and, while they summon all creatures to praise God, cannot be proved to have reference to the public worship of his house. But if they do, so far as they inculcate the use of instruments they relate to a ceremonial and typical worship.

Unless, therefore, the temple-worship, in which alone that sort of music as an accompaniment of singing in public worship was divinely authorized, can be legitimately brought over into the New Testament dispensation, the appeal to the Psalms in favor of instruments in the public worship of the Christian church is destitute of the slightest force.

In the second place, the argument from the Psalms proves too much, and is therefore worthless. In the fifty-first Psalm, which has been in all ages since its incorporation into the sacred canon a vehicle for expressing the penitential confessions of God's people, David prays: "Purge me with hyssop, and I shall be clean; wash me, and I shall be whiter than snow." The hyssop dipped into the blood of the paschal lamb was used to sprinkle the lintels and door-posts of the Israelites, as a token of their salvation from the doom which impended over the first-born of Egypt, and as a type of a greater deliverance to be afterwards accomplished by God's appointed Lamb. (Ex. xii. 21–24.) It was also employed in connection with the cleansing of the leper (Lev. xiv.), and with the burnt-sacrifice of the red heifer without the camp. (Num. xix.) In the fiftieth Psalm, the Lord, addressing Israel, says: "I will not reprove thee for thy sacrifices or thy burnt-offerings to have been continually before me;" and in the conclusion of the fifty-first, David, after praying that God would do good in his good pleasure to Zion, and build the walls of Jerusalem, exclaims: "Then shalt thou be pleased with the sacrifices of righteousness, with burnt-offering and whole burnt-offering: then shall they offer bullocks upon thine altar." While these passages partly refer to individual cleansing, it cannot be denied that they, far more clearly than those cited in favor of instrumental music, relate to the public worship of God's house. If, now, the argument holds good, which is derived from the Psalms in support of the use of instruments in the public worship of the Christian church, it equally holds in justification of the offering of bloody sacrifices in that worship. The absurdity of the consequence completely refutes the argument.

The only way in which I can conceive that an attempt may be made to evade the point of this fatal consideration, is by maintaining that the sacrifices of the ancient worship were types which have been abolished in consequence of their fulfilment by Christ, the great expiatory sacrifice, but that instrumental music was not typical, and therefore remains. One can now see why the preceding argument, to prove the typical character of instrumental music as a part of the temple worship, was so elaborately pressed, and sustained by so long a *catena* of authorities. If that argument was conclusive, this method of escape is nothing worth. Only what was generic, essential, permanent in the worship of God's ancient people passes over into the new economy; what was specific, accidental, temporary has vanished with the old; and it has been shown by conclusive proofs that to the latter kind of worship instrumental music must be assigned. It was a temporary environment by which it pleased God to surround the singing of his praise, and as typical it has been stripped away by its fulfilment in the copious effusion of the Holy Spirit, and the glorious effects of his grace in applying the accomplished atonement of Christ. We are Christians. Jews we are, if believers, "inwardly," as Paul declares; Jews as we are the spiritual seed of Abraham, and partake of his faith, as we possess, at least are entitled to possess, and possess more fully, the benefits of that unchanging covenant of grace which, in its *essential* provisions was administered in the Patriarchal and Mosaic dispensations, is administered in the Christian, and will, in the Heavenly, be administered "throughout all ages, world without end." Jews we are not, as says the same apostle, "outwardly:" Jews, not by carnal descent or national lineage, not as bound by the positive enactments of the ceremonial law, not as subject to the *accidental* provisions, the specific, peculiar, typical elements which constituted the temporary shell of that immutable covenant.

This argument from the Old Testament Scriptures proves vastly too much. Those who have most urgently insisted upon it have acted with logical consistency in importing priests into the New Testament church; and as priests suppose sacrifices, lo, the sacrifice of the Mass! Instrumental music may not seem to stand upon the same foot with that monstrous corruption, but the principle which underlies both is the same; and *that* whether we are content with a single instrument, the cornet, the bass-viol, the organ, or go on by a natural development to the orchestral art, the cathedral pomps, and all the spectacular magnificence of Rome. We are Christians, and we are untrue to Christ and to the Spirit of grace when we resort to the abrogated and forbidden ritual of the Jewish temple.

III.

Argument from the New Testament.

We have seen, by an examination of the Old Testament Scriptures, that throughout the Mosaic dispensation this great principle exerted a controlling influence: That whatsoever God commands is to be observed, and that whatsoever he does not command is forbidden, so far as the public worship of his house is concerned. Under the operation of that principle, instrumental music, as an accompaniment of the singing of praise, was excluded from the tabernacle during almost the whole period of its existence, and from the synagogue, and was introduced into the temple in consequence of a divine warrant expressly furnished to that effect. We come now to the consideration of the New Testament, and the question is, Has Christ, the King of the church, prohibited the introduction of instrumental music into its public worship? That he has will be maintained on the following grounds:

1. What was peculiar and distinctive in the worship of the Jewish temple has been abolished.

This has been the general view of the Christian church, but it has been ridiculed by infidels and opposed, in part, by some prelatists: ridiculed by the former because it supposes a change of divine enactments and infers the admission of God's mutability;[1] op-

---

[1] The answer to this is found in the obvious distinction between moral and positive laws—the former being immutable, the latter not.

posed by the latter, because they seek justification for introducing into the Christian church a class of officers and an order of worship which belonged alone to the Jewish temple. It is somewhat curious that this question is but rarely discussed in systems of theology and histories of the church. It will, therefore, not be gratuitous to state some of the reasons which justify the view, that what was peculiar to the temple-worship has been abrogated. This may be inferred from—

(1.) The nature of the case. It is conceded that some of the elements of the temple-service were typical. While the Jew denies that they have met their fulfilment in their corresponding antitypes, the Christian affirms. The latter, consequently, must hold that the types, not as objects of study, but as elements of religion to be observed, have passed away. The antitypes, as substantial realities approaching in the future, cast their shadows before them. They were dimly outlined in those shadows. When, in the process of time, the substances themselves were reached, what need was there for further following the guidance of the shadows? To take another view, indicated also by Scripture, the types were prophecies and promises presented concretely, and not merely in words, to the ancient worshipper. They were real manifestations, in the phenomenal sphere, of the purpose of redemption and of the sure Word of prophecy. But the things prophesied and promised have been actually accomplished, and are now in the possession of the Christian worshipper. History in part, and in part a continuous present experience, have taken the place of prophecy and promise. Once more, the peculiar elements of the temple-service were figurative representations of future realities, of realities not known by experience. What need of the figures when the real objects figured are experimentally known? A surveyor's plat or a topographical map is of utmost value to one who expects to purchase, but cannot inspect, a tract of land. When he is in actual possession of it, he gazes upon it with his own eyes, and the map is no longer a necessity. A likeness of a person whom one has never seen, but desires to see, is precious until actual acquaintance ensues. Why study the picture when one looks into the face of the person himself? From the nature of the case, then, the distinctive elements of the temple-worship have passed away. They have expired by their own limitation.

(2.) The statements of Scripture. Let us follow the order of the New Testament writings, and select some of the testimonies which they furnish.

First, We encounter the song of Simeon, who, when he had taken the infant Jesus into his arms, "blessed God, and said, Lord, now lettest thou thy servant depart in peace, according to thy word: for mine eyes have seen thy salvation;" and the words of the prophetess Anna, who "gave thanks likewise unto the Lord, and spake of him [Jesus] to all them that looked for redemption in Jerusalem."

Secondly, The Baptist, pointing to Jesus as with the index-finger of the old economy, exclaimed, "Behold, the Lamb of God, which taketh away the sin of the world." Look! there he is, God's provided and appointed Lamb, the great atoning sacrifice, who was typified by every lamb sacrificed at the tabernacle and the temple.

Thirdly, "Philip findeth Nathanael, and saith unto him, We have found him, of whom Moses in the law, and the Prophets, did write, Jesus of Nazareth, the son of Joseph." And when Nathanael, convinced of his Messiahship, uttered the confession, "Rabbi, thou art the Son of God; thou art the King of Israel," Jesus received the confession and confirmed the testimony.

Fourthly, "After that John was put in prison, Jesus came into Galilee, preaching the gospel of the kingdom of God, and saying, The time is fulfilled, and the kingdom of God is at hand." Again he said, "Neither do men put new wine into old bottles: else the bottles break, and the wine runneth out, and the bottles perish: but they put new wine into new bottles, and both are preserved;" by which he evidently taught that, as the new dispensation was about to begin, its spirit would transcend the forms of the old, and necessitate their abrogation. In his dying words, "It is finished," Jesus, in actually fulfilling the types of the old economy, pronounced them abolished. His whole mediatorial work on earth was completed, and all the figures of it were superseded by the reality. After his resurrection, in rebuke of the unbelief of his disciples, he said, "O fools and slow of heart to believe all that the prophets have spoken: ought not Christ to have suffered these things, and to enter into his glory? And beginning at Moses, and all the prophets, he expounded unto them in all the Scriptures the things concerning himself."

There are three aspects in which the necessity which Christ here affirms for his sufferings and glorification may be regarded. First, there was an absolute necessity, on the supposition of a free determination on

God's part to save sinners, that a competent atonement for their guilt should ground their reconciliation to him, consistently with his infinite perfections—his justice, truth and holiness. Secondly, there was a necessity that the legal substitute who would die for the expiation of guilt should be a priest, not only to evince with perfect clearness his own free and cheerful susception of the great undertaking, and to be qualified by actual experience to sympathize with his people in suffering, but also to provide, by the offices of an infinitely meritorious Minister of worship, for the access of sinners to God, and the acceptance of their prayers and their praises. But, thirdly, there was a necessity for a fulfilment of the types and prophecies of the Old Testament, and there can be but little doubt that it was chiefly upon this point that the Lord Jesus insisted, in his talk with the disciples on their way to Emmaus. The legal and ceremonial institutions of Moses and the promissory writings of the prophets he expounded as having had reference to himself, and therefore virtually declared that they had all been fulfilled, so far as they related to his sufferings and atoning work, or were in process of fulfilment, so far as they pointed to his entrance into his glory—his ascension to heaven, his session on the throne, his intercession, his communication of the Holy Spirit, and his second coming to complete the redemption of his people and to judge the quick and the dead. But a promise fulfilled ceases to be a promise, and a type realized in its antitype is a type no more: its prospective office necessarily expires. It is evident, therefore, from the discourse ascribed by the evangelist to our Lord, that the peculiar and distinctive elements of the temple-worship, so far as they figured a future atonement by priestly sacrifice, had been abrogated, and so far as they represented a future effusion of the Holy Ghost soon would be abrogated.

Fifthly, On the day of Pentecost Peter declared that the wonderful outpouring of the Holy Spirit which was then experienced was in fulfilment of a prophecy of Joel. That fulfilment the apostolic preacher explained by saying: "This Jesus hath God raised up, whereof we are all witnesses. Therefore being by the right hand of God exalted, and having received of the Father the promise of the Holy Ghost, he hath shed forth this which ye do now see and hear." Now, not only were the death and glorification of Christ conjoined with the effusion of the Spirit in the prophecies, but they were also associated with each other in the temple types. Both classes of prospective representations, the prophetical and the typical, in this their twofold significance, were fulfilled. We have seen, moreover, that the feast of Pentecost, which was a constituent element of the temple-services, was typical of the copious effusion of the Holy Spirit, and it was precisely on the day of Pentecost that it met a conspicuous fulfilment. What are we to conclude, but that as the types of Christ's death and exaltation had necessarily expired, the same was true of those which pre-figured the outpouring of the Holy Ghost? In answer to this it may be said that the prophecy cited by Peter had only a partial, however glorious, fulfilment on the day of Pentecost, and continues to be a prediction of copious effusions of the Spirit, and so the temple-services which bear upon the same continuous impartation of his grace may be legitimately employed until the consummation shall be reached. What is true of the prophecies may be true of the types.

But, in the first place, the same would hold good with reference to the continued prosecution of Christ's intercessory work in heaven. Now, that was certainly typified by the high-priestly offering of incense in the Jewish holy of holies. The argument, if worth anything, would avail to show that the typical representations of Christ's intercession may still be retained in the church. What would be the consequence? This: that so much of the temple-service as typified the sacrificial death of Christ was abrogated and has vanished, and so much as pertained to his intercession, as not yet completed, may still be legitimately employed. That is to say, a service which God made one great whole, may now, at the discretion of the church, be divided in twain—a part discarded and a part retained. No sober Protestant mind could possibly entertain such a view. No more, for like reasons, could it tolerate a retention of those typical services which foreshadowed the continuous effusion of the Holy Ghost. Either the whole temple-service or none: these are the alternatives to which the Christian church was reduced. It elected the latter, and it has been reserved for Rome and the high-church Prelatists who agree with her to pursue a middle course, and not presuming to retain bloody sacrifices, to divorce what God had joined together, and to perpetrate the solemn mockery of a mutilated temple ritual.

In the second place, the temple itself was a type of Christ and his mediatorial work. But it has fulfilled its typical office, and has ceased to exist. To retain a part of its services is to suppose the continued existence of the temple, for God never authorized the employment of those services except in immediate connection with that particular structure, after the tabernacle had given way to it by his inspired direction. The force of this consideration is acknowledged by the Jews themselves, who do not pretend to offer bloody sacrifices elsewhere. If the cathedral takes the place of the temple, we would have many sacred edifices, in many different places, substituted for the only temple which existed by divine appointment, to which the tribes of Israel and proselytes from distant countries repaired to celebrate the great typical festivals. If we may have but one substitute for it, which one? Shall it be St. Peter's? And must all the world go to that mountain to worship, when Jesus Christ has said that neither at Mount Gerizim nor at Mount Moriah will men be obliged to worship? Jesus has thus declared that the positive enactment which required ceremonial worship at the Jewish temple is abrogated; and the New Testament is utterly silent in regard to any transfer to the Christian church of the services peculiar to that edifice.

In the third place, although the prophecies contained in the Old Testament taught a continuous communication of the Spirit until the complete establishment of Christ's mediatorial kingdom on earth, yet they themselves were finished when they were uttered. So with the types foreshadowing the same thing. We might as warrantably add to those prophecies new predictions because they have not had a consummate fulfilment, as continue to employ the types because they have not had an exhaustive realization. Both sorts of prospective representations were limited by God's will, and the attempt to reinstitute either, or to continue either, by the will of man, would be to invade God's prerogative and to disobey God's authority.

In the fourth place, the effusion of the Holy Spirit has already in the past been in part enjoyed by the church, and is in part now enjoyed by the church, and to perpetuate services which typify it, would be at one and the same time to confound a type which has reference to the future with a symbol commemorating the past, and to observe the type at the very time that the antitype is actually manifested. In either case contradiction and absurdity would result. The truth is, that the glorious, though partial, fulfilment of the prophecies and types alike of the old dispensation constitutes a pledge, definite and sufficient, of their exhaustive fulfilment in the future. If it be said that the New Testament contains prophecies of its own touching the future progress of Christ's kingdom, the reply is easy, that they were finished and sealed up with the completion of the sacred canon, and that unless the church has the right, furnished by fresh inspiration, to create substantive additions to the Scriptures which God pronounces perfect, she has no authority to utter prophecies, in the strict sense, any more; and it may be asked, where are the types peculiar to the New Testament? Are we pointed to baptism and the Lord's supper? Let it be proved that they are types at all; and if that could be proved, all that would be established is that the church is restricted to them alone, and the plea for a sacerdotal ritual of typical services would be cut up by the roots.

To all this it may be answered, that what is contended for is that the Christian church is warranted by the observance of services analogous to those of the Jewish temple to *commemorate* the past illustrious events of her history. Where is the warrant? We have a divine warrant for the observance of the Lord's day. We have a divine warrant for the observance of the two sacraments of baptism and the Lord's supper. What other days are we enjoined to keep holy? What other symbolical ordinances are we commanded to observe? To take the ground that the church has a discretionary power to appoint other holy days and other symbolical rites is to concede to Rome the legitimacy of her five superfluous sacraments and all her self-devised paraphernalia of sacred festivals. There is no middle ground. Either we are bound by the Lord's appointments in his Word, or human discretion is logically entitled to the full-blown license of Rome.

Sixthly, The speech of Stephen before the Jewish Council. This speech of the illustrious proto-martyr of the Christian church must ever be regarded as one of the strongest scriptural proofs of the abolition of the temple-worship; but as it will come to be considered as one of the elements in the direct argument against the use of instrumental music in public worship, its examination will for the present be deferred.

Seventhly, The decree of the Synod of Jerusalem. Certain Judaizing teachers who went from Judea to Antioch "taught the brethren, and said, Except ye be circumcised after the manner of Moses, ye cannot be saved." This raised the whole question about conformity to the institutions of the ceremonial law by the Christian church. That question was referred to the decision of the apostles and elders at Jerusalem. Paul and Barnabas were the commissioners. They laid the case before an assembled synod. The decree of that body, which was sent to the Gentile churches, was: "That ye abstain from meats offered to idols, and from blood, and from things strangled, and from fornication: from which if ye keep yourselves, ye shall do well. Fare ye well." The significant absence of any allusion, explicitly made, to the question about the ceremonial law was manifestly equivalent to a decision that it was not necessary that the churches should conform to the requirements of that law. It was tantamount to a judgment that the Mosaic institutions, so far as they were ceremonial and typical, were no longer binding. Of course, it follows that the venerable synod regarded the observance of the temple-worship as no longer obligatory, and discharged the Gentile churches from the duty of adhering to any of its elements which were distinctive of the old dispensation.[1] To suppose that those churches, after such a discharge, had discretionary power to retain the services of the ceremonial code is to suppose that they might, at discretion, forsake the liberty they had in Christ and resume the yoke of Moses. The supposition is absurd. As the great body

---

[1] This was afterwards expressly asserted to Paul by the apostles at Jerusalem as the sense of the synod's decision. "As touching the Gentiles," said they, "which believe, we have written and concluded that they observe no such thing." Acts xxi. 25.

of the Christian church has been gathered from the Gentiles, the inference is obvious.

Eighthly, The speeches of Paul at his last visit to Jerusalem. The charge which was brought against him was this: "This is the man that teacheth all men everywhere against the people, and the law, and this place." If the charge had been even partly false that he taught against the law and the temple, Paul's first step in his defence would evidently have consisted in denying it. This denial he did not make. How can the fact be accounted for, except upon the ground that Paul was well aware that both the temple and its peculiar services were doomed? He knew the prediction of Jesus that the building would be destroyed, and he had special reason for remembering the defence of Stephen before the Council, in which that servant of Christ contended that the whole typical ritual would give way to the sublime simplicity of worship which would characterize the new dispensation. That Paul himself occasionally worshipped *at the temple* was a mere matter of expediency. That he took part in its ceremonial and typical observances there is no proof to show. Indeed, without any assertion upon the subject, may not the question be raised, whether, after the day of Pentecost, when the Christian dispensation was inaugurated, the apostles did not, *as men*, commit a mistake in worshipping at all at the temple. It is difficult to believe that Stephen worshipped there.

Ninthly, The argument in the Epistle to the Hebrews is decisive. In the first place, it shows that the Aaronic priests and Levitical ministers have vanished, having been superseded by a priest after the order of Melchizedek, who has offered a perfect sacrifice, and lives forever to intercede for his people and consummate the work of redemption. If there be no priests and Levites to officiate, how is it possible to continue the services of the temple? To say that they are succeeded by Christian ministers is flatly to contradict the argument of the inspired writer. In the second place, the argument expressly proves that the temple-worship has been abolished. After stating the fact that the first covenant [that is, the Jewish dispensation[1]] had "ordinances of divine service and a worldly sanctuary," and specifying the things contained and the offices performed in the latter, it declares that "the first tabernacle"—and by this term the temple, as well as the tabernacle proper, was designated—"was a figure for the time then present;" but that Christ had come, "a high priest of good things to come by a greater and more perfect tabernacle." The figure had been realized in that which was figured, and consequently there was no longer any necessity for its teaching; indeed, its teaching would be utterly false and misleading. In the third place, the argument shows that the ceremonial law, as a mere shadow of good things to come, was inefficacious to provide for the removal of guilt from the conscience and the sanctification of the soul. But these ends are now secured by Christ through the sacrifice of himself. Now there is no need to approach God by

---

[1] The allusion here cannot be to the covenant of works as historically preceding the covenant of grace. It is to that special form in which God administered the covenant of grace in the Jewish dispensation which gave way to another form of administration under the Christian economy.

the old way of the temple-worship. We are at liberty to approach him by a new and living way, which Christ hath consecrated for us through the veil; that is to say, his flesh. His atoning death has cancelled the necessity for the temple and all its ceremonial and typical observances.

(3.) The providence of God settled this question. It effectually abolished the temple and its services. The Lord Jesus, before his death, predicted the destruction of the temple itself. Forty years after his death the Romans destroyed it. This, it may be urged, proved nothing as to the legitimacy of continuing its services: it may, for aught we know, be restored. It is true that the temple was rebuilt after the Babylonish captivity. This was accomplished upon the expiration of seventy years only, and then by God's direction. The Messiah had not come, and the typical office of the temple might still be fitly discharged. But he did come, and the rending of the veil, when he expired, was the patent signal of the temple's doom. More than eighteen hundred years have elapsed since its destruction, and it is not yet rebuilt. God has never directed its reconstruction, but on the contrary has by his providence prevented it when it has been attempted. The Emperor Julian, commonly called the Apostate, made the effort, and was baffled in a most extraordinary way. In speaking of what he terms "the miraculous interposition of heaven, which defeated Julian's attempt to rebuild the Jewish temple of Jerusalem," Bishop Warburton says: "Sacrifices constituting the essentials of their [the Jews'] worship, their religion could not be said to exist longer than that celebration continued. But sacrifices were to be performed in no place out of the walls of their temple. So that when this holy place was finally destroyed, according to the prophetical predictions, the institution itself became abolished. Nor was anything more consonant to the genius of this religion, than the assigning such a celebration of its principal rites. The temple would exist while they remained a people, and continued sovereign. And when their sovereignty was lost, the temple-worship became precarious, and subject to the arbitrary pleasure of their masters. They destroyed this temple: but it was not till it had lost its use. For the rites, directed to be there celebrated, were relative to them only as a free-policied people.

"So that this was, in reality, a total *extinction* of the Jewish worship. How wonderful are the ways of God! This came to pass at that very period when a new revelation from heaven concurred with the blind transactions of civil policy, to supersede the law by the introduction of the gospel: the last great work which completed the scheme of human redemption.

"To confound this admirable order of providence was what induced the Emperor Julian to attempt the rebuilding of the Jewish temple of Jerusalem. The vanity of the attempt could only be equalled by its impiety; for it was designed to give the lie to God, who, by the mouth of his prophets, had foretold that it should never be rebuilt. Here, then, was the most important occasion for a miraculous interposition, as it was to defeat this mad attempt. And thus in fact it was defeated, to the admiration of all mankind.

"But as a large and full account of the whole affair hath been already given to the public, in a work entituled—Julian, or a Discourse concerning the Earthquake and Fiery Eruption which defeated that Emperor's attempt to rebuild the Temple at Jerusalem; thither will I refer the learned reader, who will there meet with all the various evidence of the fact, abundantly sufficient to support and establish it; together with a full confutation of all the cavils opposed to its certainty and necessity."

It may be pleaded, that although the temple may be irrevocably destroyed, its priestly services may, in some sense, be transferred in a modified form and under new conditions to the Christian church: that the New Testament itself authorizes the offices of a priesthood. Yes, it declares all believers to be made priests in Christ to God, but priests, as offering eucharistic sacrifices—sacrifices of themselves, of their prayers, and of their substance. Nothing more need be said in rebuttal of this wretched perversion of Scripture than that the word *priest* (ἱερεύς) is never, in the singular, applied in the New Testament to any merely human officer of the church. He who assumes to be officially a priest usurps the prerogative of Jesus Christ, and audaciously invokes his judgment. This is sufficient in reply to sacerdotalists who, if not already within the pale of Rome, need only to push out their views to a legitimate conclusion in order to reach the popish outrage of the Mass.

We must concur with Warburton in holding that the destruction of the temple, after the death of Christ, involved the "extinction" of all that was peculiar and characteristic in the temple-worship.

The abolition of the temple-worship, so far as it was peculiar to the Jewish dispensation, has now been proved by an appeal to the nature of the case, to the statements of the New Testament Scriptures, and to the awful providence of God; and as it was before incontestably shown that instrumental music was employed alone in that worship, so far as the public religious services of God's people were concerned, it follows that that kind of music is, with those limitations, abolished, and that its use in the Christian church is contrary to the Word and will of God.

2. The second argument will be derived from the reproduction by the Christian church, under New Testament conditions, of the essential principles of polity and worship which obtained in the Jewish synagogue.

Let us pause to indicate briefly the elements of difference and of similarity between the church of the new dispensation and that of the old.

The prominent elements by which the Christian church was obviously distinguished from the Jewish were:

(1.) The actual advent, death, resurrection, exaltation, intercession, and mediatorial reign, of Christ; with all the consequences which flowed from those stupendous events. The old church looked forward to them all; the new looks backward to some of them, contemplates others as continuing to exist, and looks ever forward to the *second* coming of the Saviour to complete the redemption of his people and judge the quick and the dead. Jesus is more distinctly, than was possible to the Old Testament saints, recognized and worshipped as the King and Head of the church, and as the Mediatorial Sovereign to whose hands God the Father has committed dominion over all things in heaven, earth and hell.

(2.) The influence proceeding from the copious effusion of the Holy Spirit, and the results attending it, upon the disciples and their fellow-believers in wonderfully increasing their gifts and graces, and upon the mass of unbelievers in the conviction of their minds and the conversion of their souls.

(3.) The elimination of all that was ceremonial and typical in the old dispensation. Only two symbolical ordinances are commanded by Christ to be observed: the sacraments of baptism and the Lord's supper. Simplicity is the reigning genius of worship, only such external instrumentalities being allowed as are necessary to constitute the media of its expression. All else, save baptism and the Lord's supper, is swept away.

(4.) The exaltation, accentuation and extension of the preaching function: evangelism is made dominant in contradistinction to the dominant conservatism of the Old Testament church,—dominant, let it be observed, for the Jewish church was not merely and absolutely conservative, as provision was made for the admission of proselytes from the Gentile nations; and the Christian church is very far from being simply evangelistic, since it is an important part of her duty to preserve, maintain and defend the truth, and to train the sons of God for service on earth and glory in heaven.

(5.) The emphasizing of the singing of praise in public worship. There is reason to believe that the apostles made singing, as a distinct and articulate part of worship, more prominent in the Christian church than it had been in the services of the Jewish synagogue. The reason would seem to be plain. It is the most fitting vehicle for the utterance of gratitude and joy; and the Christian is peculiarly called upon to express these sentiments in worship, in consequence of the finished atonement of Christ and the out-poured influence of the Holy Ghost.

The question next being, what elements of similarity there are between the church under the new dispensation and that under the old, it is obvious from what has been said in regard to the typical and temporary character of the Jewish temple, that it could not have constituted the pattern or model in conformity with which the Christian church was organized. We must look elsewhere, if anywhere, for such an ideal. We find that in the Jewish synagogue, as an organized institute, there existed those essential elements of polity and worship which possess the character of permanence, elements which were destined to form the abiding attributes of the visible church through all dispensational changes. We might, therefore, conclude, from the very nature of the case, that such elements would pass over by an easy transition, without the jar of dislocation and a wholly new construction, to the church of the new dispensation. This antecedent presumption we discover to be confirmed by facts.

The synagogue, according to those authors, both Jewish and Christian, who are best entitled to speak on the subject, had, as to its polity, elders, deacons, and—I am disposed to believe—preachers. At least, there was the germ of the preaching function which only needed expansion to make it complete. Here were the essential elements, which only required to be modified by New Testament conditions to become the constituents of the polity and order of Christian congregations. When, accordingly, the majority of a Jewish synagogue were converted to the Christian faith, it became at once, simply by a profession of Christianity, without any marked outward change, a Christian church, with its officers already in existence, and consequently not needing to be elected and ordained. In a word, there was no necessity to create new offices. The old might need to be modified and extended in consequence of the new relations and conditions involved, but not to be vacated so that new offices, another kind of offices, should be substituted for them. Hence, in the accounts given in the Acts of the Apostles of the first gathering of Christian churches, we have no notice of the institution of the office of elder *ab initio*. The Jewish elders of the synagogue became the Christian elders of the church. The same, with the exception of the apostles and other extraordinary officers, would seem to have been true of all the offices of the Christian church—of preachers, and in all probability of deacons. There is no positive proof that the appointment of the Seven was a creation of the diaconal office. The evidence tends to an opposite conclusion. The narrative leads naturally to the conclusion that there were, under the superintendence of the apostles, Hebrew deacons who attended to the distribution of the common fund contributed by the church; and that the Seven (whose names are Hellenistic), were added to the already existing corps of deacons, in order to still the murmurs of the Hellenist converts and adequately meet their wants. As this is a point only subsidiary to the argument in hand, it will not be elaborately discussed. A considerable mass of testimonies might be collected from learned writers who, although characterized by different types of theological and ecclesiastical thought, have contended that the Christian church was organized after the analogy of the synagogue. It may be sufficient to cite the frequently quoted remarks of one who, in view of his church relations and official position, must be regarded as having spoken with distinguished candor upon this subject. "It is probable," says Archbishop Whately,[1] "that one cause, humanly speaking, why we find in the Sacred Books less information concerning the Christian ministry and the constitution of church-governments than we otherwise might have found, is that these institutions had less of novelty than some would at first sight suppose, and that many portions of them did not wholly originate with the apostles. It appears highly probable—I might say, morally certain—that, wherever a Jewish synagogue existed, that was brought, the whole, or the chief part of it, to embrace the gospel, the apostles did not there so much form a Christian church (or congregation, *ecclesia*), as make an existing congregation Christian, by introducing the Christian sacraments and worship, and establishing whatever regulations were requisite for the newly-adopted faith; leaving the machinery (if I may so speak) of government unchanged; the rulers of synagogues, elders and other officers (whether spiritual or ecclesiastical, or both) being already provided in the

---

[1] *Kingdom of Christ*, pp. 83-85. Am. Ed., pp. 84-86.

existing institutions. And it is likely that several of the earliest Christian churches did originate in this way; that is, that they were converted synagogues, which became Christian churches as soon as the members, or the main part of the members, acknowledged Jesus as the Messiah.

"The attempt to effect this conversion of a Jewish synagogue into a Christian church seems always to have been made, in the first instance, in every place where there was an opening for it. Even after the call of the idolatrous Gentiles, it appears plainly to have been the practice of the apostles Paul and Barnabas, when they came to any city where there was a synagogue, to go thither first and deliver their sacred message to the Jews and 'devout Gentiles'; according to their own expression (Acts xiii. 17), 'to the men of Israel and those that feared God;' adding that 'it was necessary that the Word of God should first be preached to them.' And when they founded a church in any of those cities in which (and such were, probably, a very large majority) there was no Jewish synagogue that received the gospel, it is likely they would still conform, in a great measure, to the same model." In these views such men as Grotius, Vitringa, Selden and Lightfoot concur.

If this be so, if the Christian church adopted its polity and its ordinary officers from the Jewish synagogue, it is almost unnecessary to argue that it appropriated its mode of worship from the same source. It was that to which in the past the people of God had been accustomed in their stated meetings on the Sabbath. Why should it not have continued for all the future? This would have been the almost inevitable result, unless the Head of the Church had authoritatively directed a change to be made, and had prescribed another and a different method of worship which he willed to be observed. There is not the slightest proof to show that he did, except in the instances of baptism and the Lord's supper; and this silence of Christ, and the absence of inspired direction to that effect by the Holy Ghost, are entitled to be construed as an approval of the continuance by the church of the long-standing and venerable mode of worship of the Jewish synagogue. This probable argument amounts to certainty, in view of the significant fact, that the elements of public worship actually enumerated in the New Testament are precisely those which existed in the synagogue. As, then, the use of instrumental music was unknown in the worship of the synagogue it was not introduced into the Christian church.

To this two considerations may be added: first, that the analogy between the synagogue and the Christian church is sustained by the fact that the LXX. frequently use the term *ecclesia* as convertible with synagogue; and secondly, that as the temple stood and its worship continued for many years after the first Christian churches were constituted, the introduction into them of a kind of music which every Jew knew to be peculiar to the temple would have furnished in itself a reason for intense hostility to Christianity, and have called forth a special opposition which would have left its impress upon the records of the times, both sacred and profane. But we hear nothing of such a conflict, and the inference is well-nigh irresistible that the ground for it did not exist; instrumental music had no place in the early Christian churches. This particular consideration is, moreover, enhanced when we reflect that the Jewish synagogues themselves passed by an easy transition into Christian congregations. But that the converted Jew should, without difficulty, have admitted into the synagogue, even though christianized, an element which belonged to the temple as peculiar and typical, or that the Christian should have adopted part of a worship the abolition of which he knew to be certain, is either of them a supposition too violent to be entertained.

3. The third argument against the employment of instrumental music in the Christian church will be drawn from the great speech of Stephen before the Jewish Council.

He was altogether an extraordinary man. Endowed with great intellectual abilities, full of faith and power and of the Holy Ghost, he disputed with such vigor against the Libertines, Cyrenians and Alexandrians, and them of Cilicia and Asia, that "they were not able to resist the wisdom and the spirit by which he spake." The reference to Cilicia makes it highly probable that in these public discussions he had Saul, the scholar of Tarsus and the disciple of Gamaliel, as one of his antagonists; and it may be that the defeat in argument to which the gifted and aspiring zealot was subjected may have armed him with the acrimony which found so conspicuous expression at the execution of the martyr. Not being able to cope with him on the field of honorable debate, his adversaries resorted to the expedient which discomfited malice is wont to suggest—they prosecuted him before the supreme judicatory. The charge against him was: "We have heard him speak blasphemous words against Moses and against God; this man ceaseth not to speak blasphemous words against this holy place, and the law: for we have heard him say that this Jesus of Nazareth shall destroy this place, and change the customs which Moses delivered us." As is apt to be the case, this charge is partly true and partly false. It was false, so far as it alleged blasphemy against Moses and against God. So far as it affirmed Stephen's declaration, that the temple would be destroyed, and the customs or rites, as ceremonial and typical, of the Mosaic code, would be changed, it must, for two reasons, be considered true—in the first place, because the defendant never denied that allegation; and in the second place, because his defence itself proved its relevancy. This construction of the charge has strong support. "This charge," says Prof. Joseph Addison Alexander,[1] "was no doubt true, so far as it related to the doctrine that the new religion, or rather the new form of the church, was to supersede the old." "Down to this time," observes Dr. Arthur Penrhyn Stanley,[2] "the apostles and the early Christian community had clung in their worship, not merely to the holy land and the holy city, but to the holy place of the temple. This local worship, with the Jewish customs belonging to it, he [Stephen] now denounced. So we must infer from the accusations brought against him, confirmed as they are by the tenor of his defence. The actual words of the charge may have been false, as the sinister and malignant in-

---

[1] *Comm. on Acts*, Chap. vi.   [2] *Art. Stephen*, Smith's Dict. of Bible.

tention which they ascribed to him was undoubtedly false. 'Blasphemous,' that is, 'calumnious' words, 'against Moses and against God' he is not likely to have used. But the overthrow of the temple, the cessation of the the Mosaic ritual, is no more than St. Paul preached openly, or than is implied in Stephen's own speech: 'against this holy place and the law—that Jesus of Nazareth shall destroy this place, and shall change the customs that Moses delivered us.'"

The speech, in conformity with a tendency of the oriental mind, is cast in the framework of an historical statement, and to the cursory reader does not present the features of an argument. It is nevertheless a powerful argument. There are two great principles the assertion of which it involved, and upon which it proceeded: first, the spirituality of God; secondly, his infinite immensity. From the first the great speaker argued that it would be folly to hold that God could be adequately worshipped by material emblems and ceremonial rites. From the second he derived the consequence that as God could not be confined to one place, neither could his worship. These positions he sustained by an appeal, in the first place, to the history of Israel, and, in the second place, to the doctrine of the prophets. He shows that the church-state of the Hebrews had undergone great changes—changes which rendered it impossible that they could have worshipped always in one particular mode, in one particular locality, and at one particular sanctuary. The church, as organized in the family of their great ancestor, Abraham, worshipped without the temple. The church, while in bondage in Egypt, worshipped without the temple.

The church, in its migrations for forty years in the wilderness, worshipped without the temple. The church, after it had found rest in the land of promise, through the whole period of the Judges, and through the reigns of Saul and David, worshipped without the temple. It was not until Solomon that the temple was built, and its peculiar services were inaugurated as supplementary to, and perfective of, those which had belonged to the tabernacle. Here Stephen reaches the conclusion of the first branch of his argument—namely, that the history of the Hebrew church proved that the temple in which his judges gloried had not been, in the past, a necessity to the spiritual worship of God, and therefore it involved neither absurdity nor impiety to hold that the church would again worship without it.

He then proceeds to confirm this lesson from the Israelitish history by the doctrine of the prophets, which teaches the greatness, majesty, infinity of God: "Howbeit the Most High dwelleth not in temples made with hands; as saith the prophet, Heaven is my throne, and earth is my footstool: what house will ye build me? saith the Lord: or what is the place of my rest? Hath not my hand made all these things?" Evidently the argument went to show the unreasonableness of so localizing the worship of the infinite Being as to tie him to a single house of worship. It implicitly affirmed the temporary character of the temple, and would, in all probability, have made the assertion explicit had not some manifestation of anger and pride on the part of the Council interrupted the speaker. This led the fearless and impassioned witness for the gospel directly to indict his judges: "Ye stiff-necked and uncircumcised in heart and ears, ye do always resist the Holy Ghost: as your fathers did, so do ye." It is clearly implied that as their fathers had resisted the Holy Ghost in respect to the matter of worshipping according to God's appointments, so *they* resisted him in the same manner. When, for example, the Spirit directed their fathers to worship at the temple, they worshipped on high places and in groves. Now that a new dispensation had been introduced, and the Holy Ghost directed them to abandon the temple-worship as having discharged its typical and temporary office, they disobeyed him, and insisted upon continuing that worship. This outburst of holy eloquence cut them to the heart and drew from them expressions of rage. And when he declared that he saw Jesus, whom he had charged them with having murdered, standing on the right hand of God, it became intolerable, and resolving themselves into a furious mob, they rushed upon him, dragged him outside the gate of the city, and pitilessly stoned him to death.

In this speech it is clear that Stephen erected a testimony which cost him his life in favor of the abrogation of the temple-worship; and as instrumental music was peculiar to that worship, we have an independent line of proof from the New Testament that it was not introduced, and was not designed to be introduced, into the Christian church.

There is, besides, another aspect of this immortal speech which must not be overlooked. Stephen, endowed with extraordinary penetration of mind, and with a wonderful inspiration of the Holy Ghost, seemed to be in advance of the apostolic college itself in his estimate of the genius of gospel-worship. He contended, as the Lord Jesus had before declared, that the spirituality of God demanded spiritual worship, and delivered a testimony sealed with blood in behalf of the absolute simplicity of gospel institutions. Stripped of all the burdensome though splendid ritual of the temple, they would reproduce the simple and unostentatious services of the synagogue, and interject nothing which was not expressly prescribed by divine authority, or required by necessity, between the living worshipper and the living God. *The spirituality and simplicity of gospel-worship*,—this was what the illustrious deacon insisted upon in burning words and with dauntless spirit before that bigoted and furious bench of zealots; this was the principle which he saturated with martyr blood at the very beginning of the Christian dispensation. Would that every officer of the church would imitate the glorious example, and in the face of popular clamor and the demands of this world's princes, bear an unwavering testimony against the introduction into the public worship of the church of *every* abrogated element of the ancient temple-services!

4. The next proof is based upon the teaching of Christ and his apostles—a teaching enforced by their practice.

(1.) The teaching of the Lord Jesus excluded instrumental music from the public worship of the New Testament church. He declared that God is vainly worshipped when the doctrines and commandments of men are substituted for his own. We have seen that, by divine direction, by the doctrine and commandment of God, instrumental music in the Old Testament church was excluded from the ordinary, stated worship of his people on the Sabbath day in the synagogue, and was confined to the services of the temple. We have also seen that the Christian church in its polity and worship was, under the conditions and with the modifications necessitated by the new dispensation, modelled after the Jewish synagogue. No entirely new element of worship was incorporated into the services of that church. Jesus did not authorize the effectuation of such a change. Consequently the introduction of instrumental music, which God had not sanctioned, or rather had prohibited, in the worship of the synagogue would have been the substitution of a doctrine and commandment of men for those which proceeded from God.

In his conversation with the Samaritan woman at Jacob's well, our Saviour enounced the great principle of the spirituality of worship: "God is a spirit, and they that worship him must worship him in spirit and in truth." While he acknowledged that the Jews, in contradistinction to the Samaritans, paid intelligent worship to God, for the reason that it involved the knowledge of salvation—a salvation to be accomplished by One who, according to the flesh, would spring from the Jewish stock, and while he virtually admitted that they had complied with divine direction in conducting a ceremonial and typical worship with its seat at Jerusalem, he added the significant words: "Believe me, the hour cometh, when ye shall neither in this mountain, nor yet at Jerusalem, worship the Father. . . . . The hour cometh and now is, when the true worshippers shall worship the Father in spirit and in truth:

for the Father seeketh such to worship him." In these words, which adumbrated the genius of gospel-worship, our blessed Lord clearly taught two things: first, that the ceremonial, typical, ritualistic worship of the Jewish temple was designed to be temporary, and that the hour was swiftly approaching when it would be entirely abolished; secondly, that even that stated worship which had been devoid of a ceremonial, typical and ritualistic character, would, under the influences to be exerted upon the people of God in the dispensation about to be inaugurated, become more spiritual than ever. These lessons the Lord Jesus manifestly inculcated, and they justify the inferences: that as instrumental music was a peculiar appendage of the temple it would pass away with it; and that, as it was absent from the synagogue, the Christian church, which was destined to be more spiritual in its worship than was even that unceremonial and untypical institute, could not consistently with its advanced nature and office introduce it into its services. It would suppose in the church of the New Testament a lower degree of spirituality in worship than was possessed by that of the Old.

Furthermore, our Lord, in issuing to his apostles, just before his ascension to glory, the great commission which contemplated the evangelization of the world, imposed upon them this solemn obligation: "Teaching them to observe all things whatsoever I have commanded you." This injunction of the Prophet and King of the church involved three things: first, that the apostles, in their oral communications and in their inspired writings, were to teach all those things which Christ commanded; secondly, that they were to teach nothing but what Christ commanded; and thirdly, that the church to be organized by them was to obey their teaching, originated and enforced by the authority of Christ, and to introduce nothing into her doctrine, polity and worship which was not either expressly or impliedly warranted by the command of Christ as reflected by apostolic inculcation and example. This left the church no discretion in regard to these elements of doctrine, government and worship. She is absolutely bound by Christ's commands, enounced originally by the lips of the apostles, and now permanently recorded in his inspired Word. She is obliged to do all that he has commanded; she is forbidden to do anything which he has not commanded. She can construct no new doctrine, institute no new element of government, and decree no new rites and ceremonies—introduce no new mode of worship. The inquiry, what discretionary power the church possesses in the sphere of worship, will be reserved to another part of this discussion. It is sufficient now to say, that it is a discretionary power which she is never entitled to use *as the church*, but simply as an organization acting under secular and temporal conditions belonging to all human societies. It is only where there is no need, perhaps no room, for a command of Christ—in the sphere in which human wisdom, the natural judgment of men, is competent to act, in which indeed it must act, it is only here that the church is, from the very necessity of the case, invested with discretionary power.

The question now being, Did Christ command the use of instrumental music in his church? the answer must be, He did not. There is certainly no such command on record. Nor can it be presumed. The Lord Jesus knew the divine decree by which the temporary services of the temple were destined to be abolished. He himself predicted the utter destruction of the temple. He knew perfectly that instrumental music was an attachment to the peculiar and distinctive services of the temple, and therefore he knew that it must share the wreck to which the temple with all those services was doomed. Did he authorize his church to save instrumental music from the ruins, and employ it in her worship? He did not. Is she then warranted to do it? Assuredly not.

Our Lord, as a man, was perfectly familiar with the worship of the synagogue. It is said that there were in his day at least four hundred and fifty synagogues in the great city of Jerusalem itself, churches in which the population worshipped from Sabbath to Sabbath, just as a Christian people now worship in theirs. His custom was to attend the synagogue wherever in his blessed itinerancy he chanced to be. He full well knew the absence of instrumental music from its services, and he knew that his church, when established as such, would follow the precedents of stated Sabbath worship, which reached immemorially back through the history of his ancient people. Did he leave a command to his church to depart from that order, and introduce instrumental music into its stated Sabbath worship? He did not; and the defect of such a command is sufficient to settle the question.

These considerations, did they need confirmation, would find it in the actual practice of our Lord. We are informed that he sang psalms with his disciples.

On the fatal night in which he was betrayed, he closed the affecting solemnity of instituting the sacrament of the supper with singing. "And when they had sung an hymn," say two of the evangelists in identically the same language, "they went out into the Mount of Olives;" and the writer of the Epistle to the Hebrews, in the wonderful chapter in which he argues the necessity of the incarnation—the community of nature betwixt Christ and his brethren, touchingly portrays him as discharging the office of their preacher and of their precentor, saying, "I will declare thy name unto my brethren, in the midst of the church will I sing praise unto thee." Nothing do we hear of instruments of music; but, as Justin Martyr, or the pseudo-Justin, says of the psalmody of the early church, only "simple singing." De Quincey[1] has contemptuously represented the singing of the English Dissenters "as a howling wilderness of psalmody." He might have spared his ridicule, had he reflected that one of the clerks who have led that kind of singing was Jesus Christ himself. But "vain man would be wise, though man be born like a wild ass's colt." He has, with magnificent rhetoric, described "the swell of the anthem, the burst of the hallelujah chorus, the storm, the trampling movement of the choral passion, . . . the tumult of the choir, the wrath of the organ." Perchance he wrote better than he knew, when he represented the organ as bringing forth wrath; and his prelatical scorn for Christ's humble and obedient people, as well as his splendid rhetoric in glorifying the pomps of cathedral-

---

[1] *Writings*, Vol. i. p. 224; Boston: Ticknor, Reed and Fields, 1851.

service, may be offsetted by the following passage from the coryphæus of British liberty:[2] "In times of opposition, when either against new heresies arising, or old corruptions to be reformed, this cool unpassionate mildness of positive wisdom is not enough to damp and astonish the proud resistance of carnal and false doctors, then (that I may have leave to soar awhile as poets use) Zeal, whose substance is ethereal, arming in complete diamond, ascends his fiery chariot drawn with two blazing meteors, figured like beasts out of a higher breed than any the zodiac yields, resembling two of those four which Ezekiel and St. John saw; the one visaged like a lion, to express power, high authority and indignation, the other of countenance like a man, to cast derision and scorn upon perverse and fraudulent seducers: with these the invincible warrior, Zeal, shaking loosely the slack reins, drives over the heads of scarlet prelates, and such as are insolent to maintain traditions, bruising their stiff necks under his flaming wheels." Or, we may listen to the rolling thunder of a mightier rhetoric than De Quincey or Milton wielded—a thunder that, like the angry growl of a coming storm, preludes the doom of that apostate mother from whose fertile womb have crept the monstrous corruptions which have slimed the purity of Christ's fair and glorious bride: "Babylon the great is fallen, is fallen, and is become the habitation of devils, and the hold of every foul spirit, and a cage of every unclean and hateful bird. . . . Alas, alas, that great city, that was clothed in fine linen, and purple, and scarlet, and decked with

---

[2] Milton's *Prose Works*. Vol. i., p. 135; Philadelphia: John W. Moore. 1847.

gold, and precious stones, and pearls! . . . Rejoice over her, thou heaven, and ye holy apostles and prophets; for God hath avenged you on her. . . . And the voice of harpers, and of musicians, and of pipers, and trumpeters, shall be heard no more in thee. . . . And after these things I heard a great voice of much people in heaven, saying, Alleluia; salvation, and glory, and honor, and power, unto the Lord our God: for true and righteous are his judgments: for he hath judged the great whore, which did corrupt the earth with her fornication, and hath avenged the blood of his servants at her hand. And again they said, Alleluia. And her smoke rose up forever and ever."

(2.) The teaching of the apostles excluded instrumental music from the public worship of the church.

Among the parts of that worship which are enumerated in the New Testament the singing of praise is included, but not instrumental music. The passages which are relevant are: 1 Cor. xiv. 26: "How is it then, brethren? when ye come together, every one of you hath a psalm, hath a doctrine, hath a tongue, hath a revelation, hath an interpretation. Let all things be done unto edifying." Eph. v. 19: "Speaking to yourselves in psalms and hymns and spiritual songs, singing and making melody in your hearts to the Lord." Col. iii. 16: "Teaching and admonishing one another in psalms and hymns and spiritual songs, singing with grace in your hearts to the Lord."

"The cause of all the contention," says the Rev. A. Cromar,[1] "is in the fact, that the word *psalm* and the word translated *making melody*, suggest at once to the

---

[1] *Vindication of the Organ*, pp. 93, 94.

mind the idea of instrumental music. A psalm is with propriety defined, a sacred ode designed to be sung to the accompaniment of the lyre, and the word rendered *making melody* literally signifies, to strike the string of the same instrument. Taking the words in their simplicity, the passage, as far as music is concerned, seems to consist of two parts—the one enjoining the *general* duty of praise in compositions sung either with or without an instrumental accompaniment; and the other *particularly* stating that praise, whether it be *with* or *without* instrumental guidance, must always be of true gospel character, that is, must be an exercise of the heart. If this, the most *probable*, be also the *true*, sense of the passage (Eph. v. 19); then we have in it what the friends of the organ believe to be the divine mind in the matter."

The weight of scholarly authority is certainly against Mr. Cromar, and those who, like him, would twist these passages to the support of instrumental music in the public worship of the church. Dr. James Begg, in noticing the exception taken by an anonymous writer to our translation of the Bible, and his affirmation, with others, that ψάλλω radically signifies playing on a stringed musical instrument, has these remarks which are worthy of attention :[1] "This attempt to fix the meaning of the word as implying playing instead of singing, as used by the New Testament writers, was thoroughly set aside by Dr. Porteous, by a variety of evidence, one part of which is thus concluded: 'From these quotations from the Greek fathers, the three first of whom flourished in the fourth century—men of great erudi-

---

[1] *The Use of Organs*, p. 264, ff.

tion, well skilled in the phraseology and language of Scripture, perfectly masters of the Greek tongue, which was then written and spoken with purity in the countries where they resided; men, too, who for conscience sake would not handle the Word of God deceitfully, it is evident that the Greek word $\psi άλλω$ signified in their time singing with the voice alone. Had they conceived otherwise, we may be assured that they had both sufficient firmness of mind and influence in the church to have induced their hearers to have used the harp and psaltery in the public worship of God.'

"It is curious to observe how constantly, and with what pretence of learning, mistakes are repeated. In a late discussion, the correctness of our authorized translation of James v. 13 was confidently called in question, and it was affirmed that $\psi αλλέτω$ meant to strike as on the lyre, and that the passage ought not to have been translated 'let him sing psalms,' but 'let him play on an instrument.' The issue thus raised is a very broad and important one, being neither more nor less than whether instrumental music is divinely appointed in Christian worship. It indicates, at all events, how far some hymnologists are prepared to go. If this idea is correct, the Christian church in the early ages had entirely mistaken the meaning of inspired men, and so has our church [the Scottish] since the Reformation. We affirm, however, that $\psi αλλέτω$ in James can mean nothing else than 'let him sing psalms.' The substantive $\psi αλμός$ occurs not oftener than *seven* times in the New Testament; and its use there, apart from other evidence, would be sufficient to determine the meaning of the verb $\psi άλλω$. The noun occurs *three* times (Luke

xx. 42, xxiv. 44; Acts i. 20), where it refers to the book of Psalms; *once* (Acts xiii. 33), where it refers to the second psalm; *twice* (Eph. v. 19; Col. iii. 16), where with other two words the rendering is 'psalms, hymns, and spiritual songs'; and *once* (1 Cor. xiv. 26), 'When ye come together, every one of you hath a psalm.' In regard to the verb itself, besides the passage in James and in Ephesians v. 19, just referred to, ψάλλω only occurs *three* times in the New Testament; *twice* (1 Cor. xiv. 15), where its use absolutely excludes instrumental music, and must imply singing inspired (?) songs or psalms—'I will sing with the spirit, and I will sing with the understanding also;' and *once* (Rom. xv. 9), 'As it is written, For this cause I will confess to thee among the Gentiles, and sing unto thy name.' It is interesting to notice that the latter passage is exactly copied from the Septuagint (Ps. xviii. 49), and this affords a striking proof of the correctness of the rendering for which we are now contending. As thus quoted by the apostle, we have an inspired rendering into the Greek verb ψάλλω of a Hebrew word which is usually translated 'sing praises' or 'sing psalms.' 'Singing psalms' was the only authorized vocal praise of the church of old. The question now, as every one knows, is not about the roots or the original meaning of words, but about the sense in which they were used by the inspired writers; ψάλλω never occurs in the New Testament, in its radical signification, to strike or play upon an instrument.

"The forty or fifty high scholars of England through whose hands the authorized version of our Scriptures passed, were thoroughly acquainted with these things, and seldom fail, in matters of the least importance, to give, either in the text or in the margin, a correct version of the original language—although, of course, they were not infallible. In connection with this, it is not uninteresting, however, to observe how fully the correctness of our authorized version is confirmed by Luther and the early Reformers. Luther translates ψαλλέτω (Jam. v. 13) 'der singe psalmen;' Wickliffe, 'and seye he a salm;' Tyndale, 'let him singe psalmes;' and Cranmer, 'let him synge psalms.' Dean Alford, too, among recent critics, strong Episcopalian as he is, and interested in vindicating instrumental music, renders the word 'let him sing praise.' Mr. Young, in his translation of the Bible 'according to the letter and idioms of the original languages,' renders the passage, 'let him sing psalms;' and Dr. Giles, late Fellow of Christ Church College, Oxford, in his New Testament, 'translated word for word,' London, 1861, also renders it, 'let him sing psalms.'"

There is no need to multiply authorities. All commentators admit that psalms primarily designated sacred odes which were suited to be accompanied, when sung, by instruments of music. But the great majority concur in holding that the secondary sense, of sacred compositions to be sung, is that in which the word is used in the New Testament. How could it be otherwise with men who had learning enough to know, that instrumental music was excluded from the public worship of the apostolic church? If it be urged that this is begging the question, and proof be demanded, the appeal is taken, first, to the preceding argument; and, secondly, to the practice of the post-apostolic church.

If the apostles had allowed the employment of instrumental music in the church, it is morally certain, from the very constitution of human nature, that it would have continued to be used subsequently to their time. But it was not; and its absence can be accounted for only on the ground that the New Testament Church had never adopted it. If it had been in use under the apostles, its ejection could only have been accomplished by a revolutionary change which would have been a revolt from apostolic practice. Such a supposition is on every account absurd—indeed is impossible. The proof that the early church knew nothing of instrumental music it is proposed to furnish in a subsequent part of this discussion. Its presentation is, therefore, postponed.

Even if the foregoing argument from the New Testament Scriptures had only a respectable degree of probability, it would seem to be preposterous to attempt its refutation by a single ambiguous word—a word conceded by those who take that position themselves to have both an original and a secondary signification. As, further, it is not pleaded that the words "*hymns and spiritual songs*" imply the accompaniment of instruments, they who stand on the primary sense of the word *psalms* would be obliged to admit that some of the singing of the apostolic church was accompanied by instrumental music and some was not. When they succeed in proving that such was the case, they may with some plausibility claim the surrender of their opponents. Is it not evident that the argument which rests on the single word *psalms* swings on a rickety hinge?

5. The only other argument from the New Testament Scriptures will be derived from the condemnation which they pronounce upon "will-worship." Will-worship is that which is not commanded by God, but devised by man. We have seen that God commanded instrumental music to be employed in connection with the temple. It was, therefore, in that relation not an element of will-worship. It was of course legitimate. But had the Jew employed it in the synagogue, he would have been guilty of the sin of will-worship. Why? Because, without the divine warrant he would have asserted his own will in regard to the public worship of God. Now that the temple is gone, all that was peculiar to it is gone with it. To revive any of its defunct services, and borrow them from its ruins for the ornamentation of the Christian church, is an instance of will-worship. The general principle is enounced by Paul in the Epistle to the Colossians, although he applies it specifically to a certain class of cases. "Wherefore," says he, "if ye be dead with Christ from the rudiments of the world, why, as though living in the world, are ye subject to ordinances, (Touch not; taste not; handle not; which are all to perish with the using;) after the commandments and doctrines of men? which things have indeed a shew of wisdom in will-worship, and humility, and neglecting of the body; not in any honor to the satisfying of the flesh." Instrumental music, as has been proved, was one of the rudiments of that ceremonial and typical ritual by which it pleased God to train the Israelites, as children in a preparatory school, for the manhood of the Christian dispensation with its glorious privileges and its expanded

responsibilities. This was the view of even Aquinas and Bellarmin. He, therefore, who would import that effete element into the Church of the New Dispensation would impugn the wisdom of God, assert his will against the divine authority, and abandon the freedom of Christ for the bondage of Moses.

IV.

Argument from the Presbyterian Standards.

In arguing against the use of instrumental music in public worship from the Presbyterian standards—that is, the formularies of doctrine, government and worship of the Presbyterian Church—I desire it to be distinctly understood that they are not viewed or treated as an authority independent of the inspired Word of God. All the authority which they possess—every whit of it—is derived from that Word. Apart from it they have none. In the first place, as human compositions they may or may not exactly accord with the Scriptures and faithfully represent their meaning. So far as they do, and only so far as they do, they are clothed with the authority of the divine Word itself, and as every Christian admits that the authority of that Word is binding upon all men, they, to that extent, confessedly exercise a controlling authority upon all men. In the second place, the members, and especially the officers of that church of which they are a directory of faith and practice, are, over and beyond this general obligation which rests upon all men, under a special obligation resulting from their voluntary acceptance of these standards as a true interpretation of the Scriptures, and from their covenanted agreement with their brethren of the same faith and order to be governed by them as the constitution of their church. It is, therefore, with reference to them, not exclusively, but in a very special sense, that, in the construction and development of this particular argument, the appeal is made to the Presbyterian standards. I speak as unto wise men; let them judge what may be said in relation to this venerable tribunal.

Let it be also noticed that, in pursuing this particular line of argument, it is by no means claimed that new material proofs are derived from these formularies. The proofs have already been presented from the Scriptures, both of the Old Testament and of the New, and the conclusion which they justify has already been reached and enounced. The present appeal is to the standards as clearly summing up the scriptural proofs and definitely enforcing the conclusion, and as having a peculiar authority for those who, in the conflict of religious opinions, have adopted them as, in their judgment, a correct statement and exposition of the law of the Lord. But in addition to this, let it be remarked, these standards clearly define the limitations upon such discretionary power in the sphere of worship, and in every other sphere, as is to be conceded to the church. They define it both negatively—declaring what it is not; and positively—declaring what it is; and it is in this especial regard that the reference to their authority is invested with interest and importance.

1. Instrumental music is, by good and necessary consequence, excluded from the public worship of the church by the exposition which the Catechisms furnish of the Second Commandment. In the citation of their words, only such will be adduced as bear upon the subject of worship and are relevant to the question in hand.

"What," asks the Larger Catechism,[1] "are the duties required in the second commandment?" "The duties required in the second commandment are the receiving, observing, and keeping pure and entire all such religious worship and ordinances as God hath instituted in his Word. . . . Also, the disapproving, detesting, opposing all false worship, and, according to each one's place and calling, removing it."

"What are the sins forbidden in the second commandment?" "The sins forbidden in the second commandment are: All devising, counselling, commanding, using, and any wise approving any religious worship not instituted by God himself; . . . all superstitious devices, corrupting the worship of God, adding to it or taking from it, whether invented and taken up of ourselves or received by tradition from others, though under the title of antiquity, custom, devotion, good intent, or any other pretence whatsoever; . . . all neglect, contempt, hindering, and opposing the worship and ordinances which God hath appointed."

"What are the reasons annexed to the second commandment, the more to enforce it?" "The reasons annexed to the second commandment, the more to enforce it, contained in these words, For I the Lord thy God am a jealous God, visiting the iniquity of the fathers upon the children unto the third and fourth generation of them that hate me: and showing mercy unto thousands of them that love me and keep my commandments; are, besides God's sovereignty over us and propriety in us, his fervent zeal for his own worship, and his revengeful indignation against all false

---

[1] Questions 108, 109, 110.

worship, as being a spiritual whoredom; accounting the breakers of this commandment such as hate him, and threatening to punish them unto divers generations, and esteeming the observers of it such as love him and keep his commandments, and promising mercy to them unto many generations."

The Shorter Catechism[1] thus condenses these statements of the Larger: "The second commandment requireth the receiving, observing and keeping pure and entire all such religious worship and ordinances as God hath appointed in his Word." It "forbiddeth the worshipping of God by images, or any other way not appointed in his Word." "The reasons annexed . . . are, God's sovereignty over us, his propriety in us, and the zeal he hath to his own worship."

Let us attentively consider the features of this commandment which are signalized by these formularies:

(1.) The zeal and jealousy, fervent and lasting, which God manifests touching everything that concerns his worship. This is suited to arrest our notice, and to alarm and restrain those who assert their right to decree rites and ceremonies, and to regulate divine worship according to their own judgment and taste as to what is fitting and decorous in the services of the Lord's house. He himself stands guard over his own sanctuary, and, armed with bolts of vengeance, threatens with condign punishment the invaders of his prerogative, the usurpers of his rights. We have seen how awfully this lesson was enforced under the old dispensation, how swiftly, like lightning, his judgments flashed against rash and insolent assertors of their own will in regard

---

[1] Questions 50, 51, 52.

to the mode in which he was to be worshipped, and how severely he dealt with his own choicest and holiest servants for departures from his prescriptions in this matter. This vehement zeal and jealousy of God for the purity of his worship should deter us from venturing one step beyond the directions of his Word. Who, for the sake of the ornaments of art and the suggestions of fancy, would unnecessarily challenge the visitations of his wrath? In this dispensation he is patient and forbearing, but who will coolly elect to go, with the unexpunged guilt of encroaching upon the sovereignty of God over the worship of his house, to the tremendous bar of last accounts?

(2.) The great principle is here brought out and emphasized, that not only is what God has positively commanded to be obeyed, but what he has not commanded is forbidden. The law is, not that we are at liberty to act when God has not spoken, but just the contrary: we have no right to act when he is silent. It will not answer to say in justification of some element of worship that God has not expressly prohibited it; we must produce a divine warrant for it. The absence of such a warrant is an interdiction. The exposition of the second commandment enforces the obligation, not only to receive, observe and keep pure and entire all such religious worship and ordinances as God *hath instituted* in his Word, but also not to devise, counsel, command, use and any wise approve any religious worship *not instituted* by God himself. The instance, already commented on, of Nadab and Abihu, the sons of Aaron, God's venerable high priest, is exactly in point. They were visited with summary judgment, as we are explicitly told, for performing a function in worship which God had not commanded. We cannot without guilt transcend divine appointments. No discretion is allowed the church to introduce into public worship what God himself has not instituted and appointed. He has not constituted her his vicegerent or his confidential agent. She is intrusted with no powers plenipotentiary. She acts under instructions, and is required to adhere to the text of her commission.

The application to instrumental music in the public worship of the church is plain. It was permissible, as has been shown, only when God commanded it, and he commanded it in connection with the typical and temporary services of the temple. He did not command it to be used in the ordinary Sabbath worship of the synagogue, and accordingly it was not employed in that institute. The Jew obeyed the divine will in that respect. God did not command it to be introduced into the Christian church, and in conformity with his will it was not employed in the apostolic or the early church. It was not known in the church for centuries. It was, as will be shown, a late importation into its services—an importation effected without divine authorization, and therefore in the face of the divine will. If our exposition of the second commandment is valid—and we acknowledge it to be both valid and authoritative—we violate that commandment when we employ instrumental music in public worship, because we devise, counsel, command, use and approve a mode of "religious worship not instituted by God himself." That God did not institute it, either in connection with the Jewish synagogue or with the Christian church, has been irrefragably proved.

These things being so, we cannot, in accordance with the requirements of this commandment, acquiesce in the employment of instrumental music in the public worship of the church. No "title of antiquity, custom, devotion, good intent, or any other pretence whatsoever," will justify or excuse us. It will not avail us to plead that we found it in use, and are not called upon to urge or enact revolutionary measures. We are bound to disapprove, detest, oppose all false worship, and as this is in that category, to disapprove, detest and oppose it. The argument to prove its want of divine warrant must be overthrown before the position of inaction and acquiescence can be conscientiously maintained. Nor will it do to say that we have not examined the question—that we do not know. We ought to examine, we ought to know, for as Presbyterians our standards plainly expound to us the divine law on the subject, and as Christians we have no right to be ignorant of the teaching of Scripture in regard to it. "To the law and to the testimony; if they speak not according to them, it is because there is no light in them."

The principle, thus strongly emphasized by the exposition of the second commandment, that a divine warrant is required for everything entering into the worship of God, is also enounced and enforced in the following utterances of the Confession of Faith: "God alone is Lord of the conscience, and hath left it free from the doctrines and commandments of men which are in any thing contrary to his Word, *or beside it* in matters of faith and worship."[1] "The acceptable way of worshipping the true God is instituted by himself, and so limited by his own revealed will, that he may not be worshipped according to the imaginations and devices of men, or the suggestions of Satan, under any visible representation, *or any other way not prescribed in the Holy Scripture.*"[2] In these words the Confession declares, that the conscience is left free to reject the teaching of any doctrines and the authority of any commandments which are beside the Word of God in the matter of worship; and that it is not permissible to worship him in any way not prescribed in the Scriptures. If, as has been evinced, instrumental music in public worship was in the Old Testament only prescribed as an appendage of the temple, and was not prescribed in connection with the synagogue, and is not prescribed in the New Testament, it is obviously beside the Word of God, destitute of his authority, and therefore to be rejected.

2. Instrumental music is excluded from the public worship of God's house by the declarations of the Confession of Faith and the Directory for Worship concerning singing.

The Confession of Faith, in enumerating the "parts of the ordinary religious worship of God," specifies "singing of psalms with grace in the heart." The Directory for Worship thus speaks: "It is the duty of Christians to praise God by singing psalms." "The proportion of the time of public worship to be spent in singing is left to the prudence of every minister."

(1.) These provisions of the Confession of Faith and

---

[1] Chap. xx., sec. 2. [2] Chap. xxi., sec. 1.

the Directory for Worship exclude instrumental music from the public worship of the church which acknowledges them as its formularies, in accordance with the legal maxim, *Expressio unius est exclusio alterius:* the express statement of one alternative is the exclusion of the other. If two men were supposed, upon probable grounds, to be chargeable with the same offence, the indictment of only one of them would be the exclusion of the other from the indictment. No formal naming of the person not included in the indictment is necessary. If of two acts, which might be performed under given circumstances, one only is commanded in a statute to be done, the other is excluded—it is not commanded. And so, if of two acts which might be done under given circumstances, one only is by statute permitted, the other is excluded from the permission—it is forbidden. To apply the principle to the case in hand: the singing of psalms or hymns and the performance of instrumental music are two distinct acts which may be done at one and the same time. The ecclesiastical law commands only one of these acts to be done in public worship. It follows that the other is excluded—it is not commanded. But does this, it may be asked, rule out the other? May it not be done, although not commanded? The answer is to be found in the great principle, already established by scriptural proofs, that what Christ has not commanded to be observed, men have no right to introduce into the worship of his church; and those who acknowledge the ecclesiastical law which is now appealed to, as correctly representing or rather reproducing the divine law, are bound to hold that what the ecclesiastical law does not authorize cannot be legitimately introduced into the worship of the church. We have seen that it is not true that what is not forbidden is permitted, but on the contrary, what is not commanded is forbidden. It follows that, as the law in the Presbyterian standards does authorize singing and does not authorize instrumental music, the latter is excluded. It is extra-legal, and therefore contra-legal.

(2.) This interpretation of the law in the standards is confirmed by what we know of the mind and intention of its framers in regard to this matter. Before the Westminister Assembly of Divines undertook the office of preparing a Directory for Worship, the Parliament had authoritatively adopted measures looking to the removal of organs, along with other remains of Popery, from the churches of England. On the 20th of May, 1644, the commissioners from Scotland wrote to the General Assembly of their church and made the following statement among others: "We cannot but admire the good hand of God in the great things done here already, particularly that the covenant, the foundation of the whole work, is taken, Prelacy and the whole train thereof extirpated, the service-book in many places forsaken, plain and powerful preaching set up, many colleges in Cambridge provided with such ministers as are most zealous of the best reformation, altars removed, the communion in some places given at the table with sitting, the great organs at Paul's and Peter's in Westminster taken down, images and many other monuments of idolatry defaced and abolished, the Chapel Royal at Whitehall purged and reformed; and all by authority, in a quiet manner, at noon-day, without tumult."[1] So thorough was the work of removing organs that the "Encyclopædia Britannica" says that "at the Revolution most of the organs in England had been destroyed."[2]

When, therefore, the Assembly addressed itself to the task of framing a Directory for Worship, it found itself confronted by a condition of the churches of Great Britain in which the singing of psalms without instrumental accompaniment almost universally prevailed. In prescribing, consequently, the singing of psalms without making any allusion to the restoration of instrumental music, it must, in all fairness, be construed to specify the simple singing of praise as a part of public worship. The question, moreover, is settled by the consideration that had any debate occurred as to the propriety of allowing the use of instrumental music, the Scottish commissioners would have vehemently and uncompromisingly opposed that measure. But Lightfoot, who was a member of the Assembly, in his "Journal of its Proceedings"[3] tells us: "This morning we fell upon the Directory for singing of psalms; and, in a short time, we finished it." He says that the only point upon which the Scottish commissioners had some discussion was the reading of the Psalms line by line.

If anything were lacking to confirm these views, it would be found in what is known of the state of opinion in the Puritan party, the party represented in the Westminster Assembly, as well before as during the sessions of that body.

---

[1] *Acts of Assembly of Church of Scotland*, 1644. [2] Art., *Organ*.
[3] *Works*, Vol. xiii., pp. 343, 344 : London, 1825.

"Her Majesty [Elizabeth] was afraid," says Neal, "of reforming too far; she was desirous to retain images in churches, crucifixes and crosses, vocal and instrumental music, with all the old popish garments; it is not, therefore, to be wondered that, in reviewing the liturgy of King Edward, no alterations were made in favor of those who now began to be called Puritans, from their attempting a purer form of worship and discipline than had as yet been established."[1]

"Drs. Humphreys and Samson," says the same historian, "two heads of the Non-conformists, wrote to Zurich the following reasons against wearing the habits." After giving the reasons the writers continue: "But the dispute is not only about a cap and surplice; there are other grievances which ought to be redressed or dispensed with; as (1) music and organs in divine worship," etc.[2]

He further says: "They [the Puritans] disallowed of the cathedral mode of worship; of singing their prayers, and of the antiphone or chanting of the Psalms by turns, which the ecclesiastical commissioners in King Edward the Sixth's time advised the laying aside. Nor did they approve of musical instruments, as trumpets, organs, etc., which were not in use in the church for above 1200 years after Christ."[3]

John Owen, the great Puritan divine, who was contemporary with the Westminster Assembly, says:[4] "Not only hereby the praising and blessing of God, but the use of those forms in so doing became a neces-

---

[1] *Hist. Puritans*, Vol. i, p. 76, Choules's ed., New York, 1863.
[2] *Ibid.*, p. 93.   [3] *Ibid.*, p. 107.
[4] *Works*, Vol. xv., p. 37, Goold's ed.

sary part of the worship of God; and so was the use of organs and the like instruments of music, which respect that manner of praising him which God then required." He speaks here of the temple-service in the Jewish dispensation. This venerable servant of Christ also says:[2] "And he [David] speaks expressly, in 1 Chron. xxiii. 5, of praising God with instruments of music 'which,' says he, 'I made.' He did it by the direction of the Spirit of God; otherwise he ought not to have done it; for so it is said, 1 Ch. xxviii. 12, when he had established all the ordinances of the temple, 'the pattern of all that he had by the Spirit.' And verse 19, 'All this,' said David, 'the Lord made me understand in writing by his hand upon me, even all the works of this pattern.' It was all revealed unto him by the Holy Spirit, without which he could have introduced nothing at all into the worship of God."

From what has been said, it is evident that the provisions in the Confession of Faith and the Directory for Worship touching singing in public worship were intended to exclude the employment of instrumental music; and it follows that its use by those who accept these formularies is in violation of their constitutional law.

3. Instrumental music is doctrinally excluded from the public worship of the church by the Confession of Faith.

The passage which is appealed to in support of this position is as follows: "The whole counsel of God con-

---

[1] *Works*, Vol. ix., p. 463.

cerning all things necessary for his own glory, man's salvation, faith, and life, is either expressly set down in Scripture, or by good and necessary consequence may be deduced from Scripture: unto which nothing is at any time to be added, whether by new revelations of the Spirit or traditions of men. Nevertheless, we acknowledge the inward illumination of the Spirit of God to be necessary for the saving understanding of such things as are revealed in the Word; and that *there are some circumstances concerning the worship of God and government of the church common to human actions and societies which are to be ordered by the light of nature and Christian prudence, according to the general rules of the Word, which are always to be observed.*"[1]

(1.) The whole preceding argument clearly proves that the Westminster Assembly could not have intended to include instrumental music in those circumstances concerning—not in, nor of, not implicated in the nature of, but concerning—the worship of God, the ordering of which it concedes not to be prescribed by Scripture, but to depend upon natural judgment and Christian discretion. Let us glance back at that argument. It proved: that the prescriptive will of God regulates all things pertaining to the kind of worship to be rendered him in his house; that nothing which is not commanded by him in his Word, either explicitly or implicitly, can be warrantably introduced into the public worship of his sanctuary; that man's will, wisdom, or taste can, in this sphere, originate nothing, authorize nothing, but that human discretion is excluded, and absolute obedience to the divine authority imposed;

---

[1] Chap. i. Sec. vi.

that instrumental music was not commanded of God to be used in connection with the tabernacle during the greater part of its existence, and consequently it was not there employed; that God expressly commanded it to be used in the temple, and therefore it was employed in its services; that the temple itself, with all that was peculiar and distinctive in its worship, was typical and symbolical, and was designed to be temporary; that it did pass away at the beginning of the Christian dispensation; that instrumental music was a part of its typical elements, and has consequently shared its abolition; that instrumental music was not commanded of God to be used in connection with the synagogue, which existed contemporaneously with the temple, and was therefore not employed in its services; that the Christian church was, in its polity and worship, conformed not to the temple, but to the synagogue, as is admitted even by some distinguished Prelatists, such modifications and conditions having been added as necessarily grew out of the change of dispensations—the accomplishment of atonement, the copious effusion of the Holy Ghost, and the evangelistic genius and office of the new economy; that instrumental music in public worship was not one of these Christian modifications or conditions; that the New Testament Scriptures exclude that kind of music, and that it was unknown in the practice of the apostolic church, as is evinced not only by the teaching of the apostles, but also by the absence of instrumental music from the church for more than a millennium.

Now, this was the way in which the Westminster divines, together with the whole Puritan party, were accustomed to argue, and in addition to this method of argument from Scripture, they also condemned instrumental music as one of those badges of Popery from which they contended that the church should be purged. To take the ground, then, that in the single clause in regard to "the circumstances concerning the worship of God . . . common to human actions and societies, which are to be ordered by the light of nature and Christian prudence," they meant to include instrumental music, is to maintain that in that one utterance they contradicted and subverted their whole doctrine on the subject. It would be to say that they made all their solemn contentions and cherished views upon that subject what the wise woman of Tekoah represented human life to be, "as water spilt on the ground, which cannot be gathered up again." The thing is preposterous. It cannot for a moment be supposed. One might, therefore, close the argument just here. Whatever the Assembly meant to include in the category of circumstances falling under the discretion of the church, it is absolutely certain that it was not intended to embrace in it instrumental music. But inasmuch as, notwithstanding this obtrusive fact, the clause in the Confession of Faith touching circumstances concerning the worship of God is unaccountably but commonly pleaded in justification of the employment of instrumental music in church services, I will endeavor to vindicate it from that abusive construction.

(2.) Let us determine, in the light of the instrument that we are interpreting, *what these circumstances are.*

They are expressly defined to be such as are "common to human actions and societies." It would seem needless to discuss the question. One feels that he is talking superfluously and triflingly in arguing that circumstances common to human actions are not and cannot be peculiar to church actions. It is certain that circumstances common to human societies cannot be peculiar to church societies. But these circumstances are declared to be common to human societies, to societies of all sorts—political, philosophical, scientific, literary, mercantile, agricultural, mechanical, industrial, military, and even infidel. Time and place, costume and posture, sitting or standing, and the like, are circumstances common to all societies, and therefore pertain to the church as a society. But will it be seriously maintained that instrumental music is such a circumstance? Is it common to human societies? These questions answer themselves. As instrumental music is not a circumstance common to all societies, it is not one of the circumstances specified in the Confession of Faith. It is excluded by the terms which it uses.

It may be said that, as all human societies have the right to order the circumstances in which their peculiar acts shall be performed, the church possesses this common right, and may appoint the circumstance of instrumental music as an accompaniment to its peculiar act of singing praise. How this relieves the difficulty it is impossible to see. For the Confession defines the circumstances in question to be common to human actions, and therefore common to the actions of all human societies. But it will not be contended that the action of singing praise in the worship of God belongs to all societies as such. If that action does not belong to them, no circumstances attending it can belong to them. The community of the action infers the community of the circumstances attending it. The ground of the objection is therefore swept away; there is no such action common to all societies as the singing of praise in God's worship, and consequently no such circumstance attending it as instrumental music. The action and the circumstance vanish together. If the action of singing praise belonged alike to the church and all societies there might be some color of plausibility in the plea that the church may determine the circumstances which attend it as done by herself, so far, at least, as the terms of this particular clause in the Confession of Faith are concerned. If, however, the action of singing praise in God's worship is peculiar to the church as a particular kind of society, the circumstance of instrumental music as attending it cannot be common to human actions and societies. It is therefore ruled out by the language of the Confession.

This argument is conclusive, unless it can be shown that instrumental music is a circumstance necessary to to the performance of the action—singing of praise. A simple and complete answer to this is, that for a thousand years the church sang praise without instrumental accompaniment. How then can its necessity to the singing of praise be maintained? Can a circumstance be necessary to the performance of an act, when the act *has been* performed without it, and *is now* continually, Sabbath after Sabbath, performed without it? To say that instrumental music assists in the performance of the act is to shift the issue. The question is not, Is it helpful? but, Is it necessary?

To this it must be added that this particular provision of the Confession is to be interpreted in conformity with its catholic teaching and that of its sister standards. Both represent the singing of psalms as prescribed. Both are silent about the prescription of instrumental music. Now if it could be proved that the latter is necessary to the former, the prescription of one would logically imply the prescription of the other. But we have seen that there is no such necessity. We are obliged therefore to exclude instrumental music as illegitimate, in view of the express declaration of the Confession and other standards that we are forbidden to introduce anything into the worship of God which is not prescribed. Here is a circumstance which is neither necessary nor prescribed. It cannot, therefore, be among the circumstances legitimated by the Confession.

We have now seen that the action of singing praise in the worship of God is one peculiar to the church and not common to it with all other societies, and that instrumental music is a circumstance concerning this peculiar ecclesiastical action which, therefore, cannot be common to human actions and societies. Consequently, it is not one of those circumstances which are in the discretionary power of the church, precisely as they are in the discretionary power of all societies. No circumstance peculiar to and distinctive of the church, as such, can be one of the circumstances mentioned by the Confession of Faith.

The question then returns: What are the circumstances concerning the worship of God which the church has the right to order according to the light of nature and Christian prudence? Their proper definition is, that *they are* CONDITIONS *upon which the actions of all human societies are performed,—conditions without which the actions of any society either cannot be performed at all, or cannot be performed decently and in order.*

First, They are conditions which are not peculiar to the acts of any particular society, but common to the acts of all societies. They cannot, consequently, be peculiar to the acts of the church as a particular society. But instrumental music is a condition peculiar to the act of singing praise in *some* particular churches. The conclusion is obvious. Let us take, for example, the circumstances of time and place. They condition the meeting and therefore the acts of every society. None could meet and act without the appointment of a time and a place for the assembly. This is true alike of the church and an infidel club. In this respect they are dependent upon the same conditions. Neither could meet and act without complying with this condition. This is a specimen of the Confession's circumstances which are common to human actions and societies. It is ridiculous to say that instrumental music is in such a category.

It cannot be overlooked, as has just been intimated, that instrumental music is a circumstance which is not common to even particular churches. Some have it, and some do not. How can it be common to all societies, when it is not common to churches themselves? How can the conclusion be avoided, that it is not one of the circumstances designated by the Confession of Faith?

Secondly, The circumstances indicated by the Confession are not parts of the acts of societies: they simply condition the performance of the acts. They are in no sense qualities or modes of the acts. If the proof of this position is required, it is found in the simple consideration that some at least of the acts of various societies are different acts—they are not common between them. It is therefore obvious that the parts of those acts fall into the category of the acts of which they are parts. But these circumstances are common to the acts of all societies. To recur to the example of time and place. These, it is needless to say, while necessary conditions of the acts of all societies, are, from the nature of the case, parts of the acts of none. The resolutions adopted by any society surely do not embrace in them time and place as integral elements, or qualities or modes. But instrumental music, although sometimes employed in churches by itself as a distinct act—in which case it stands confessed as not prescribed and forbidden—is generally used along with singing as a part of the act of church-worship. In these cases it certainly qualifies or modifies the act. As, therefore, it enters as an element into the acts of the church, as a distinctive society, and does not into the acts of all societies, it is ruled out by that fact from the class of cirstances indicated by the Confession.

Thirdly, These circumstances are conditions of actions as they are actions, and not as they are these or those particular kinds of actions. They condition all sorts of actions of all sorts of societies. The debates and votes of a secular deliberative body are as much conditioned by them as the prayers and praises of the church. It will scarcely be contended that instrumental music is a circumstance which conditions the debates and votes of a legislature or of a political meeting. But if not, it is conceded to be excluded from those circumstances which are pronounced by the Confession common to human actions and societies.

Fourthly, These circumstances are conditions *necessary* to the actions of all societies,—necessary either to the performance of the actions, or to their decorous performance. Let it be observed, that they are necessary not to the performance or the decorous performance of some peculiar actions of particular societies, but to all the actions of all societies. To take the ground that instrumental music is a circumstance in some way a necessary condition of the singing of praise in church-worship is to go outside of those circumstances which the Confession of Faith contemplates. A condition of this peculiar action of the church, however necessary to the performance of the action its employers may deem it, cannot possibly be a common condition of human actions and societies. It lies outside of that class, and therefore outside of the circumstances which the Confession has in view. Instrumental music is palpably such a condition, and cannot be justified by an appeal to this section of the Confession.

Fifthly, These circumstances, as conditions upon which the acts of societies are to be done, cannot be *religious* in their character. The reason is perfectly plain: they condition the acts of all secular societies, and it would be out of the question to say that they proceed upon religious conditions. But instrumental music when employed in the worship of God's house is religious. Hence the plea for organs, that they have a solemn sound, and are on that account peculiarly adapted to accompany the singing of praise as a religious act. If it be said that they are a secular accompaniment of religious worship, it may well be asked, By what right is such an accompaniment to the worship of God employed, without a distinct warrant from him? And when the organ is played without the accompaniment of the singing of praise, is it then secular or religious? If secular, will it be justified on the ground that secular music may, by itself, be allowed in God's house, and that he may be worshipped in a worldly manner? If religious, the question is given up; and then we are compelled to return to the assertion that the church has no discretion in appointing religious elements: they are not among the circumstances which are common to human actions and societies.

The foregoing argument has shown that instrumental music cannot, on any supposable ground, be regarded as a circumstance common to human actions and societies, and that it is therefore excluded by the Confession of Faith from the discretionary control of the church. Unless, then, it can be proved to be one of the things commanded by Christ and his apostles, it cannot be lawfully employed in connection with the worship of God's house. In order to meet the criticism which may be passed upon the argument that it springs from a singular and contracted conception of the doctrine as to circumstances stated in the Confession of Faith, the views of a few eminent theologians will be cited in its support.

Dr. John Owen, in arguing against a liturgy, enounces

the principles contended for in these remarks. "Circumstances," he says,[1] "are either such as follow actions as actions, or such as are arbitrarily superadded and adjoined by command unto actions, which do not of their own accord, nor naturally nor necessarily attend them. Now religious actions in the worship of God are actions still. Their religious relation doth not destroy their natural being. Those circumstances, then, which do attend such actions as actions not determined by divine institution, may be ordered, disposed of, and regulated by the prudence of men. For instance, prayer is a part of God's worship. Public prayer is so, as appointed by him. This, as it is an action to be performed by man, cannot be done without the assignment of time, and place, and sundry other things, if order and conveniency be attended to. These are circumstances that attend all actions of that nature, to be performed by a community, whether they relate to the worship of God or no. These men may, according as they see good, regulate and change as there is occasion; I mean, they may do so who are acknowledged to have power in such things. As the action cannot be without them, so their regulation is arbitrary, if they come not under some divine disposition and order, as that of time in general doth. There are also some things, which some men call circumstances also, that no way belong of themselves to the actions whereof they are said to be the circumstances, nor do attend them, but are imposed on them, or annexed unto them, by the arbitrary authority of those who take upon them to give order and rules in such cases; such as to pray

---

[1] *Works*, Vol. xv., pp. 35, 36, Goold's Ed.

before an image or towards the east, or to use this or that form of prayer in such gospel administrations, and no other. These are not circumstances attending the nature of the thing itself, but are arbitrarily superadded to the things that they are appointed to accompany. Whatever men may call such additions, they are no less parts of the whole wherein they serve than the things themselves whereunto they are adjoined." He then goes on to prove from Scripture that "such additions to or in the worship of God, besides or beyond his own institution and appointment" are not "allowable, or lawful to be practised."

In another place the same great theologian says:[1] "Whatever is of circumstance in the manner of its performance [worship], not capable of especial determination, as emerging or arising only *occasionally*, upon the doing of that which is appointed at this or that time, in this or that place, and the like, is left unto the rule of *moral prudence*, in whose observation their order doth consist. But the superaddition of ceremonies necessarily belonging neither to the institutions of worship nor unto those circumstances whose disposal falls under the rule of moral prudence, neither doth nor can add any thing unto the due order of gospel worship; so that they are altogether needless and useless in the worship of God. Neither is this the whole of the inconvenience wherewith their observance is attended; for although they are not in particular and expressly in the Scripture forbidden—for it was simply impossible that all instances wherein the wit of man might exercise its invention in such things should be reckoned up

---

[1] *Works*, Vol. xv., pp. 469, 471, Goold's ed.

and condemned—yet they fall directly under those severe prohibitions which God hath recorded to secure his worship from all such additions unto it of what sort soever. . . . The Papists say, indeed, that all *additions corrupting* the worship of God are forbidden, but such as further adorn and preserve it are not so, which implies a contradiction, for whereas every *addition* is principally a *corruption* because it is an addition, under which notion it is forbidden (and that in the worship of God which is forbidden is a corruption of it), there can be no such preserving, adorning addition, unless we allow a preserving and adorning corruption. Neither is it of more force, which is pleaded by them, that the additions which they make belong not unto the *substance* of the worship of God, but unto the *circumstances* of it; for every circumstance observed religiously, or to be observed in the worship of God, is of the substance of it, as were all those ceremonious observances of the law, which had the same respect in the prohibitions of adding, with the most weighty things whatsoever."

"There is nothing," says George Gillespie,[1] "which any way pertaineth to the worship of God left to the determination of human laws beside the mere circumstances, which neither have any holiness in them, forasmuch as they have no other use and praise in sacred than they have in civil things, nor yet were particularly determinable in Scripture, because they are infinite; but sacred, significant ceremonies, such as [the] cross, kneeling, surplice, holidays, bishopping, etc., which have no use and praise except in religion only, and

---

[1] *Works*, in Presbyterian's Armoury, Vol. i., Pref. p. xii.

which, also, were most easily determinable (yet not determined) within those bounds which the wisdom of God did set to his written Word, are such things as God never left to the determination of any human law."

He speaks more explicitly to the same effect in the following words:[1] "I direct my course straight to the dissecting of the true limits within which the church's power of enacting laws about things pertaining to the worship of God is bounded and confined, and which it may not overleap nor transgress. Three conditions I find necessarily requisite in such a thing as the church has power to prescribe by her laws:

"1. It must be only a circumstance of divine worship; no substantial part of it; no sacred, significant, and efficacious ceremony. For the order and decency left to the definition of the church, as concerning the particulars of it, comprehendeth no more but mere circumstances. . . . Though circumstances be left to the determination of the church, yet ceremonies, if we speak properly, are not . . . circumstances which have place in all moral actions, and that to the same end and purpose for which they serve in religious actions—namely, for beautifying them with that decent demeanor which the very light and law of natural reason requireth as a thing beseeming all human actions. For the church of Christ, being a society of men and women, must either observe order and decency in all the circumstances of their holy actions, time, place, person, form, etc., or else be deformed with that disorder and confusion which common reason and civility abhorreth.

---

[1] *Works*, in Presbyterian's Armoury, Vol. i., p. 130.

"2. That which the church may lawfully prescribe by her laws and ordinances, as a thing left to her determination, must be one of such things as were not determinable by Scripture on that reason which Camero hath given us, namely, because *individua* are *infinita*. . . . We say truly of those several and changeable circumstances which are left to the determination of the church, that, being almost infinite, they were not particularly determinable in Scripture. . . . . But as for other things pertaining to God's worship, which are not to be reckoned among the circumstances of it, they being in number neither many nor in change various, were most easily and conveniently determinable in Scripture. Now, since God would have his Word (which is our rule in the works of his service) not to be delivered by tradition, but to be written and sealed unto us, that by this means, for obviating satanical subtility and succoring human imbecility, we might have a more certain way for conservation of true religion, and for the instauration of it when it faileth among men,—how can we but assure ourselves that every such acceptable thing pertaining any way to religion, which was particularly and conveniently determinable in Scripture, is indeed determined in it; and consequently, that no such thing as is not a mere alterable circumstance is left to the determination of the church?

"3. If the church prescribe anything lawfully, so that she prescribe no more than she hath power given her to prescribe, her ordinance must be accompanied with some good reason and warrant given for the satisfaction of tender consciences."

"As a positive institution, with a written charter,"

remarks Dr. Thornwell,[1] "she [the church] is confined to the express or implied teachings of the Word of God, the standard of her authority and rights, . . . as in the sphere of doctrine she has no opinions, but a faith, so, in the sphere of practice, she has no expedients, but a law. Her power is solely ministerial and declarative. Her whole duty is to believe and obey. Whatever is not commanded, expressly or implicitly, is unlawful. . . . According to our view, the law of the church is the positive one of conformity with Scripture; according to the view which we condemned, it is the negative one of non-contradiction to Scripture. According to us, the church, before she can move, must not only show that she is not prohibited, she must also show that she is actually commanded, she must produce a warrant. Hence we absolutely denied that she has any discretion in relation to things not commanded. She can proclaim no laws that Christ has not ordained, institute no ceremonies which he has not appointed, create no offices which he has not prescribed, and exact no obedience which he has not enjoined. She does not enter the wide domain which he has left indifferent, and by her authority bind the conscience where he has left it free.

"But does it follow from this that she has absolutely no discretion at all? On the contrary, we distinctly and repeatedly asserted, that in the sphere of commanded things she *has* a discretion—a discretion determined by the nature of the actions, and by the divine principle that all things be done decently and in order. . . . We only limited and defined it. We never

---

[1] *Coll. Writings*, Vol.iv., p. 244, ff.

denied that the church has the right to fix the hours of public worship, the times and places of the meetings of her courts, the numbers of which they shall be composed, and the territories which each shall embrace. Our doctrine was precisely that of the Westminster standards, of John Calvin, of John Owen, of the Free Church of Scotland, and of the noble army of Puritan martyrs and confessors."

After quoting the statements of the Westminster Confession of Faith on the subject, he goes on to say: "Here the discretion is limited to *some circumstances*, and those *common to human actions and societies*. Now, the question arises, What is the nature of these circumstances? A glance at the proof-texts on which the doctrine relies enables us to answer. Circumstances are those concomitants of an action without which it either cannot be done at all, or cannot be done with decency and decorum. Public worship, for example, requires public assemblies, and in public assemblies people must appear in some costume, and assume some posture. Whether they shall shock common sentiment in their attire, or conform to common practice; whether they shall stand, sit or lie, or whether each shall be at liberty to determine his own attitude—these are circumstances; they are the necessary concomitants of the action, and the church is at liberty to regulate them. Public assemblies, moreover, cannot be held without fixing the time and place of meeting; these, too, are circumstances which the church is at liberty to regulate. Parliamentary assemblies cannot transact their business with efficiency and despatch—indeed, cannot transact it decently at all—without committees. Committees, therefore, are circumstances common to parliamentary societies, which the church, in her parliaments, is at liberty to appoint. All the details of our government in relation to the distribution of courts, the number necessary to constitute a quorum, the times of their meetings, the manner in which they shall be opened,—all these, and such like, are circumstances, which, therefore, the church has a perfect right to arrange. We must carefully distinguish between those circumstances which attend actions *as actions*—that is, without which the actions could not be, and those circumstances which, though not essential, are added as appendages. These last do not fall within the jurisdiction of the church. She has no right to appoint them. They are circumstances in the sense that they do not belong to the substance of the act. They are not circumstances in the sense that they so surround it that they cannot be separated from it. A liturgy is a circumstance of this kind, as also the sign of the cross in baptism, and bowing at the name of Jesus. Owen notes the distinction."

These great men concur in showing that the circumstances of which the Confession of Faith speaks as falling under the discretionary control of the church in the sphere of worship are not superadded appendages to the acts of worship, which may or may not accompany them as the church may determine, but are simply *conditions* necessary either to the performance of the acts or to their decent and orderly performance—conditions not peculiar to these acts of the church as a distinctive society, but common to the acts of all societies. Particular attention is challenged to the views cited from Gillespie, for the reason that he was a member of the Westminster Assembly, and of course accurately knew and expounded the doctrine of that body on this subject. He draws a clear distinction between what was determinable by Scripture and what was not. What was not so determinable was left to be determined by the church; what was so determinable was excluded from her discretion. Now it is certain that instrumental music was, under the Jewish dispensation, actually determined by the revealed will of God as an element in the temple worship. Need it be said that it was, therefore, not indeterminable? It might have pleased God to determine it as an element in the worship of the synagogue, and in like manner it might have pleased him to determine it as an appendage to that of the christian church. He did not, and consequently it is prohibited. This conclusively settles the doctrine of the Westminster Assembly. It intended to teach that instrumental music was not one of the circumstances indeterminable by Scripture and committed to the discretion of the church. As the question here is in regard to the meaning of the circumstances of which the Confession of Faith treats, this consideration is absolutely decisive. Instrumental music cannot, without violence to the Confession, be placed in the category of circumstances determinable by the church. As, then, it is not commanded it is forbidden; and they who justify its employment in public worship are liable to the serious charge of adding to "the counsel of God" which is "set down" in his Word.

V.

Historical Argument.

I hope to prove to any candid mind that the historical argument is overwhelmingly against the use of instrumental music in the public worship of the Christian church. It has already been shown that it was not employed, under the Jewish dispensation, in the tabernacle until it was about to give way to the temple, or in the stated worship of the synagogue, and that, having been by divine direction limited to the ritual of the temple, it was, along with the other distinctive elements of that temporary institute, abolished at the inauguration of the Christian economy. It has also been evinced that the Christian church, by an easy transition, carried over into the new dispensation the simple worship as well as the polity of the synagogue, modified by the conditions peculiar to that dispensation; that the employment of instrumental music in Christian worship was not one of those modifications; for such a modification would have had the effect of conforming the gospel church to the temple, with its symbolical and typical rites—a conformity from which even the synagogue was free; and that the apostles, as the divinely commissioned and inspired organizers of the New Testament church, so far from authorizing the use of instrumental music in its worship, excluded it. The Christian church, it is clear, was started without it. What has been the subsequent history of the case? In answering this question, reference will be made to the practice of the church and to the testimony of some of her leading theologians during the successive periods of her development.

There is no evidence, but the contrary, to show that instrumental music was commonly introduced into the church until the thirteenth century.

The church historians make no mention of it in their accounts of the worship of the early church. Mosheim says not a word about it. Neander makes the simple remark: "Church psalmody, also, passed over from the synagogue into the Christian church."[1] Dr. Schaff observes: "He [Christ] sanctioned by his own practice, and spiritualized, the essential elements of the Jewish cultus."[2] They were historians, and could not record a fact which did not exist.

Bingham, deservedly held in high repute as a writer on Christian antiquities, and as a member of the Anglican church certainly not prejudiced in favor of Puritan views, says:[3] "I should here have put an end to this chapter, but that some readers would be apt to reckon it an omission, that we have taken no notice of organs and bells among the utensils of the church. But the true reason is that there were no such things in use in the ancient churches for many ages. Music in churches is as ancient as the apostles, but instrumental music not so."

In regard to the doctrine of the fathers upon the subject I cannot do better than give an extract from a

---

[1] *Hist.* Vol. i., p. 304.
[2] *Hist. Apos. Ch.*, p. 345; see also *Hist. Chris. Ch.*, Vol. i., pp. 120, 121.
[3] *Works*, Vol. iii., p. 137.

learned and able work of the Rev. James Peirce,[1] entitled "*A Vindication of the Dissenters.*" "I come now," says he,[2] "to say somewhat of the antiquity of musical instruments. But that these were not used in the Christian church in the primitive times is attested by all the ancient writers with one consent. Hence they figuratively explain all the places of the Old Testament which speak of musical instruments, as I might easily show by a thousand testimonies out of Clement of Alexandria, Basil, Ambrose, Jerome, Augustin, Chrysostom, and many others. . . Chrysostom talks more handsomely: 'As the Jews praised God with all kinds of instruments, so are we commanded to praise him with all the members of our bodies, our eyes,' etc.[3] And Clement of Alexandria talks much to the same purpose.[4] Besides, the ancients thought it unlawful to use those instruments in God's worship. Thus the unknown author of a treatise among Justin Martyr's works: 'Quest. If songs were invented by unbelievers with a design of deceiving, and were appointed for those under the law, because of the childishness of their minds, why do they who have received the perfect instructions of grace, which are most contrary to the aforesaid customs, nevertheless sing in the churches just as they did who were children under the law? Ans. Plain singing is not childish, but only the singing with lifeless organs, with dancing and cymbals, etc. Whence the use of such instruments and other things fit for children is laid aside, and plain singing only retained.'[5]

---

[1] A Non-Conformist; died 1726. [2] Pt. iii., Ch. iii.; London, 1717.
[3] In Ps. cl. [4] *Pardag.*, Lib. ii., C. 4. [5] *Resp. ad Orthodox.*, Q. 107.

"Chrysostom seems to have been of the same mind, and to have thought the use of such instruments was rather allowed the Jews in consideration of their weakness, than prescribed and commanded.[1] But that he was mistaken, and that musical instruments were not only allowed the Jews, as he thought, and Isidorus of Pelusium (whose testimony I shall mention presently), but were prescribed by God, may appear from the texts of Scripture I have before referred to. Clement . . . thought these things fitter for beasts than for men.[2] And though Basil highly commends and stiffly defends the way of singing by turns; yet he thought musical instruments unprofitable and hurtful.[3] . . . He says thus: 'In such vain arts as the playing upon the harp or pipe, or dancing, as soon as the action ceases the work itself vanishes.' So that, really, according to the apostle's expression, 'the end of these things is destruction.'[4] Isidore of Pelusium, who lived since Basil, held music was allowed the Jews by God in a way of condescension to their childishness: 'If God' says he, 'bore with bloody sacrifices, because of men's childishness at that time, why should you wonder he bore with the music of a harp and a psaltery?'[5] . . . From what has been said, it appears no musical instruments were used in the pure times of the church."

2. With reference to the time when organs were first introduced into use in the Roman Catholic Church, let us hear Bingham:[6] "It is now generally agreed among

---

[1] In Ps. cl. [2] *Pædag.*, Lib. ii., C. iv., p. 163.
[3] *Comm. in Isa.*, C. v., pp. 956, 957.
[4] P. 955. [5] *Epist.*, Lib. 2, ep. 176.
[6] *Works*, Vol. iii., p. 137, ff.

learned men that the use of organs came into the church since the time of Thomas Aquinas, Anno 1250; for he, in his *Summs*, has these words: 'Our church does not use musical instruments, as harps and psalteries, to praise God withal, that she may not seem to Judaize.' From which our learned Mr. Gregory, in a peculiar dissertation that he has upon the subject, concludes that there was no ecclesiastical use of organs in his time. And the same inference is made by Cajetan and Navarre among the Romish writers. Mr. Wharton also has observed that Marinus Sanutus, who lived about the year 1290, was the first who brought the use of wind-organs into churches, whence he was surnamed Torcellus, which is the name for an organ in the Italian tongue. And about this time Durantus, in his *Rationale*, takes notice of them as received in the church; and he is the first author, as Mr. Gregory thinks, that so takes notice of them.

"The use of the instrument indeed is much more ancient, but not in church-service, the not attending to which distinction is the thing that imposes upon many writers. . . . Nor was it ever received into the Greek churches, there being no mention of an organ in all their liturgies, ancient or modern, if Mr. Gregory's judgment may be taken. But Durantus, however, contends for their antiquity, both in the Greek and Latin churches, and offers to prove it, but with ill success, first, from Julianus Halicarnassensis, a Greek writer, Anno 510, whom he makes to say that organs were used in the church in his time. But he mistakes the sense of his author, who speaks not of his own times, but of the time of Job and the Jewish temple. For, commenting on these words of Job, xxx. 31, 'My harp is turned to mourning, and my organ into the voice of them that weep,' he says: 'There was no prohibition to use musical instruments or organs, if it was done with piety, because they were used in the temple.' By which, it is plain, he speaks of the Jewish temple in the singular, and not of Christian temples or churches in the plural, as Durantus mistakes him. Next, for the Latin church, he urges the common opinion which ascribes the invention of them to Pope Vitalian, Anno 660; but his authorities for this are no better than Platina and the Pontifical, which are little to be regarded against clear evidences to the contrary. That which some urge out of Clemens Alexandrinus I shall not answer as Suicerus does, (who, with Hospinian and some, wholly decrying the use of instrumental music in Christian churches, says it is an interpolation and corruption of that ancient author,) but only observe that he speaks not of what was then in use in Christian churches, but of what might lawfully be used by any private Christians, if they were disposed to use it; which rather argues that instrumental music (the lute and harp of which he speaks) was not in use in the public churches. The same may be gathered from the words of St. Chrysostom, who says: 'It was only permitted to the Jews, as sacrifice was, for the heaviness and grossness of their souls. God condescended to their weakness, because they were lately drawn from idols; but now, instead of organs, we may use our own bodies to praise him withal.' Theodoret has many like expressions in his *Comments upon the Psalms* and other places. . . . So that, there being no use of organs till the twelfth [thirteenth?] century, I could not speak of them as utensils in the ancient churches."

Let us pause a moment to notice the fact, supported by a mass of incontrovertible evidence, that the Christian church did not employ instrumental music in its public worship for 1200 years after Christ. It proves, what has been already shown from the New Testament Scriptures, that the apostolic church did not use it in its public services, and surely the church ought now to be conformed to the practice of the apostles and of the churches whose usages they modelled according to the inspired direction of the Holy Ghost. It deserves serious consideration, moreover, that notwithstanding the ever-accelerated drift towards corruption in worship as well as in doctrine and government, the Roman Catholic Church did not adopt this corrupt practice until about the middle of the thirteenth century. This is the testimony of Aquinas, who has always been esteemed by that church as a theologian of the very first eminence, and who, of course, was perfectly acquainted with its usages. When the organ was introduced into its worship it encountered strong opposition, and made its way but slowly to general acceptance. These assuredly are facts that should profoundly impress Protestant churches. How can they adopt a practice which the Roman Church, in the year 1200, had not admitted, and the subsequent introduction of which was opposed by some of her best theologians? For example, Bellarmin, as we have already seen, condemns it as not belonging to the church perfected in the new dispensation, and Cardinal Cajetan said: "It is to be observed the church did not use organs in Thomas's time; whence, even to this day, the Church of Rome does not use them in the Pope's presence. And truly it will appear that musical instruments are not to be suffered in the ecclesiastical offices we meet together to perform for the sake of receiving internal instruction from God; and so much the rather are they to be excluded, because God's internal discipline exceeds all human disciplines, which rejected this kind of instruments."[1] The great scholar, Erasmus, who never formally withdrew from the communion of the Church of Rome, thus forcibly expresses himself: "We have brought into our churches a certain operose and theatrical music; such a confused, disorderly chattering of some words, as I hardly think was ever heard in any of the Grecian or Roman theatres. The church rings with the noise of trumpets, pipes and dulcimers; and human voices strive to bear their part with them. . . . Men run to church as to a theatre, to have their ears tickled. And for this end organ-makers are hired with great salaries, and a company of boys, who waste all their time in learning these whining tones [Ames translates, 'this gibble-gabble.'] Pray now compute how many poor people, in great extremity, might be maintained by the salaries of those singers."[2]

In spite of this opposition, the organ, during the fourteenth and fifteenth centuries, steadily made its way towards universal triumph in the Romish church. Then came the Reformation; and the question arises, How did the Reformers deal with instrumental music in the church? Did they teach that the Reformation

---

[1] Hoffm. Lex., *voce Musica*, quoted by Peirce.
[2] In 1 Cor. xiv. 19, cited by Peirce and Ames.

ought to embrace the expulsion of that kind of music from its services?

I will not appeal to Luther. Eckhard[1] is referred to as saying: "*Lutherus organa musica inter Baalis insignia refert*," "Luther considers organs among the ensigns of Baal." But the German reformer expresses a different opinion in his commentary on Amos vi. 5.

Zwingle has already been quoted to show that instrumental music was one of the shadows of the old law which has been realized in the gospel. He pronounces its employment in the present dispensation "wicked pervicacity." There is no doubt in regard to his views on the subject, which were adoped by the Swiss Reformed churches.

Calvin is very express in his condemnation of instrumental music in connection with the public worship of the Christian church. Besides the testimonies which have already been adduced to prove that he regarded it as one of the types of the Old Testament which is fulfilled in the New, other passages from his writings may be added. In his commentary on the thirty-third Psalm he says: "There is a distinction to be observed here, however, that we may not indiscriminately consider as applicable to ourselves everything which was formerly enjoined upon the Jews. I have no doubt that playing upon cymbals, touching the harp and viol, and all that kind of music, which is so frequently mentioned in the Psalms, was a part of the education—that is to say, the puerile instruction of the law. I speak of the stated service of the temple. For even now, if

---

[1] A German theologian. He argued in favor of instrumental music against Calvin.

believers choose to cheer themselves with musical instruments, they should, I think, make it their object not to dissever their cheerfulness from the praises of God. But when they frequent their sacred assemblies, musical instruments in celebrating the praises of God would be no more suitable than the burning of incense, the lighting up of lamps, and the restoration of the other shadows of the law. The Papists, therefore, have foolishly borrowed this, as well as many other things, from the Jews. Men who are fond of outward pomp may delight in that noise; but the simplicity which God recommends to us by the apostle is far more pleasing to him. Paul allows us to bless God in the public assembly of the saints, only in a known tongue (1 Cor. xiv. 16). The voice of man, although not understood by the generality, assuredly excels all inanimate instruments of music; and yet we see what Paul determines concerning speaking in an unknown tongue. What shall we then say of chanting, which fills the ears with nothing but an empty sound? Does any one object that music is very useful for awakening the minds of men and moving their hearts? I own it; but we should always take care that no corruption creep in, which might both defile the pure worship of God, and involve men in superstition. Moreover, since the Holy Spirit expressly warns us of this danger by the mouth of Paul, to proceed beyond what we are there warranted by him is not only, I must say, unadvised zeal, but wicked and perverse obstinacy."

On Psalm cl. 3–5 he says: "I do not insist upon the words in the Hebrew signifying the musical instruments; only let the reader remember that sundry different kinds are here mentioned, *which were in use under the legal economy,*" etc. On verse 6, "Let everything that hath breath praise the Lord," he remarks: "As yet the psalmist has addressed himself in his exhortations to the people who were conversant with *the ceremonies under the law;* now he turns to men in general," etc.

In his homily on 1 Sam. xviii. 1-9, he delivers himself emphatically and solemnly upon the subject: "In Popery there was a ridiculous and unsuitable imitation [of the Jews]. While they adorned their temples, and valued themselves as having made the worship of God more splendid and inviting, they employed organs, and many other such ludicrous things, by which the Word and worship of God are exceedingly profaned, the people being much more attached to those rites than to the understanding of the divine Word. We know, however, that where such understanding is not, there can be no edification, as the apostle Paul teacheth. . . . . What, therefore, was in use under the law is by no means entitled to our practice under the gospel; and these things being not only superfluous, but useless, are to be abstained from, because pure and simple modulation is sufficient for the praise of God, if it is sung with the heart and with the mouth. We know that our Lord Jesus Christ has appeared, and by his advent has abolished these legal shadows. Instrumental music, we therefore maintain, was only tolerated on account of the times and the people, because they were as boys, as the sacred Scripture speaketh, whose condition required these puerile rudiments. But in gospel times we must not have recourse to these unless we wish to destroy the evangelical perfection, and to obscure the meridian light which we enjoy in Christ our Lord."

In these views of his illustrious colleague Beza concurred.[1] "If," says he, "the apostle justly prohibits the use of unknown tongues in the church, much less would he have tolerated these artificial musical performances which are addressed to the ear alone, and seldom strike the understanding even of the performers themselves."

The French Protestant Church, which was organized mainly through the influence and counsels of Calvin, naturally adopted his views in regard to worship as well as doctrine and government. Consequently, as the Reformer did not oppose the use of a moderate and evangelical liturgy, that church following his lead employed one that was permissive, that is, not imposed by authority. One may wonder that Calvin, who unequivocally enounced the great principle that whatsoever is not commanded is forbidden, did not see the application of that principle to liturgical services, at least did not make that application practically. It would be irrelevant to the design of this discussion to consider that question as one of fact. We know that the French Reformed Church acted in accordance with his views on that subject; and it may be said, in passing, that it has been a matter of observation that the use of a liturgy by the Huguenot immigrants to this country has been a snare, which has had influence in leading many of them to abandon the church of their fathers that was so definitely opposed to prelacy, and identify themselves with a prelatic communion. Reading the case back-

---

[1] *In Colloq. Mompelg.*, Pars 2, p. 26.

ward, we can see that whatever may have been the reasons which governed the Reformer in declining to apply the mighty principle mentioned to a liturgy, they have not been sustained by events. And it is somewhat curious, at least it is a striking circumstance inviting attention to its causes, that the Scottish and American churches which are now generally opposed to a liturgy, as Calvin was not, are more and more adopting instrumental music to which he *was* opposed.

But the fact here emphasized is that the French Reformed Church, in its day of efficiency and glory, excluded instrumental music from its services. Nor is the example a mean one. It was that of a great church, as illustrious an exponent of the principles of Presbyterianism, with the exception which has just been indicated and its alliance with the state, as has existed since the days of the apostles. These principles were not worn as a uniform on parade, but were maintained through blood and flame. A few extracts from Quick's valuable work, *Synodicon in Gallia Reformata*, will illuminate this point as with a lurid glare. "Whilst," says he,[1] "Mystical Babylon, spiritual Sodom and Egypt (where our Lord hath been in his most precious truths and ordinances, and in his dearest saints and members, for many ages successively crucified), did swim in the calm ocean of worldly riches and grandeur, in the pacific seas of peculiar felicities and pleasures, poor Zion in that bloody kingdom of France hath been in the storms and flames, hath passed from one fiery trial to another, from cauldrons of boiling oil into burning furnaces heated with fire seven times hotter than before;

---

[1] *Epistle Dedicatory.*

she hath been driven from populous cities and the pleasant habitations of men unto the cold, snowy Lebanon, to the high craggy tops of Amana and Shenir, to the frightful dens of lions, and to the horrid mountains of dragons and leopards." Is this extravagant declamation? Let us glance at some of the facts.

"In the national Synod of Rochelle, in the year 1571, Mr. Beza presiding in it, the Reformed could count then above two thousand one hundred and fifty churches; and in many of these above ten thousand members, and in most of these two ministers, in some they had five, as in the year 1561 there served the church of Orleans (which at that time had seven thousand communicants) Anthony Chanoriet, Lord of Meringeau, Robert Macon, Lord des Fontaines, Hugh Sureau, Nicholas Fillon, Lord of Valls, and Daniel Tossane, who afterwards died at Heidelberg in the Palatinate. When the Colloquy [our Presbytery] of Poissy was held, they had in the one only province of Normandy three hundred and five pastors of churches, and in the province of Provence three-score. And I remember the author of *Le Cabinet du Roy de France*, a book printed in the year 1581, and dedicated to Henry the Third, makes a computation of their martyrs to have been in a very few years at least 200,000 cut off for the gospel, and he makes up his account thus: 'Allow,' saith he, 'but a hundred martyrs to every church, and you have the sum; and yet 'tis as clear as the sun at noonday that the sum is vastly more. For 'tis a truth incontestable, that there have been cut off by the sword and massacres for religion from the church of Caen above 15,000 or 16,000, from the church of Alençon 5,000, from the church of Paris 13,000 from the church of Rheims 12,000, from the church of Troyes 12,000, from the church of Sens 9,000, from the church of Orleans 8,000, from the church of Angiers 7,000, and from the church of Poictiers 12,000 persons, etc.' *Livre premier*, pp. 274-277."¹

Quick makes this remarkable statement,² which I cannot forbear quoting, concerning the powerful influence exerted by the simple singing of psalms upon the French people at the beginning of the Protestant Reformation: "Clement Marot, a courtier and a great wit, was advised by Mr. Vatablus, Regius Professor of the Hebrew tongue in the University of Paris, to consecrate his muse unto God; which counsel he embraceth and translateth fifty of David's psalms into French meter. Mr. Beza did the other hundred and all the Scripture songs. Lewis Guadimel, another Asaph or Jeduthun, a most skilful master of music, set those sweet and melodious tunes unto which they are sung even unto this day. This holy ordinance charmed the ears, hearts and affections of court and city, town and country. They were sung in the Louvre, as well as in the Prés-des-Clercs, by ladies, princes, yea, and by Henry the Second himself. This one ordinance only contributed mightily to the downfall of Popery, and the propagation of the gospel. It took so much with the genius of the nation, that all ranks and degrees of men practised it in the temples and in their families. No gentleman professing the Reformed religion would sit down at his table without praising God by singing. Yea, it was a special part of their morning and evening worship in their sev-

---

¹ *Introduction*, pp. lix., lx. ² *Ibid*, p. v.

eral houses to sing God's praises. The Popish clergy raged, and, to prevent the growth and spreading of the gospel by it, that mischievous Cardinal of Lorraine, another Elymas the sorcerer, got the odes of Horace and the filthy, obscene poems of Tibullus and Catullus to be turned into French and sung at the court. Ribaldry was his piety, and the means used by him to expel and banish the singing of divine psalms out of the profane court of France."

Whatever may be the practice in recent times of the churches of Holland, the Synods of the Reformed Dutch Church, soon after the Reformation, pronounced very decidedly against the use of instrumental music in public worship. The National Synod at Middleburg, in 1581, declared against it, and the Synod of Holland and Zealand, in 1594, adopted this strong resolution: "That they would endeavor to obtain of the magistrate the laying aside of organs, and the singing with them in the churches, even out of the time of worship, either before or after sermons." The Provincial Synod of Dort also inveighed severely against their use.

Some testimonies are added from distinguished continental theologians. Pareus, commenting on 1 Cor. xiv. 7, says: "In the Christian church the mind must be incited to spiritual joy, not by pipes and trumpets and timbrels, with which God formerly indulged his ancient people on account of the hardness of their hearts, but by psalms and hymns and spiritual songs."

"Instrumental music," remarks Zepperus,[1] "in the religious worship of the Jews, belonged to the ceremonial law, which is now abolished. It is evident that it

---

[1] *De Lege Mosaica*, Lib. iv.

is contrary to the precept and rule of Paul, who (1 Cor. xiv.) wills that in Christian assemblies everything should be done for edification, that others may understand and be reformed; so even that of speaking in unknown tongues should be banished from the church; much less should that jarring organic music, which produceth a gabbling of many voices, be allowed, with its pipes and trumpets and whistles, making our churches resound, nay, bellow and roar. . . . In some of the Reformed churches these musical instruments are retained, but they are not played until the congregation is dismissed, all the parts of divine worship being finished. And they are then used for a political [civil] purpose, to gratify those who seek pleasure from sound and harmony."

Molerus, on the 150th Psalm, observes: "It is no wonder, therefore, that such a number of musical instruments should be so heaped together; but although they were a part of the *Pædagogia Legalis* [the instruction of the law], yet they were not for that reason to be brought into Christian assemblies. For God willeth that, after the coming of Christ, his people should cultivate the hope of eternal life and the practice of true piety by very different and more simple means than these."[1]

Gisbertus Voetius argues at length against the use of instrumental music in churches in his *Ecclesiastical Polity*, a work which is held in high estimation among Presbyterians.[2] The argument is characterized by the

---

[1] The three foregoing testimonies are extracted from the report of a committee to the Presbytery of Glasgow in 1808.
[2] *Pars* i. *Cap.* iii., *De Organis et Cantu Organico in Sacris.*

great ability for which the author was noted, but it is too elaborate to be here cited.

It might seem hopeless to get from the Church of England a testimony against the employment of instruments in worship; but when her first love was warmed by the blessed influence of the reformation from Popery, she spoke in no uncertain sounds on the subject. In her homily "Of the Place and Time of Prayer" these notable words occur: "God's vengeance hath been and is daily provoked, because much wicked people pass nothing to resort to the church; either for that they are so sore blinded that they understand nothing of God or godliness, and care not with devilish example to offend their neighbors; or else for that they see the church altogether scoured of such gay, gazing sights as their gross phantasie was greatly delighted with; because they see the false religion abandoned and the true restored, which seemeth an unsavory thing to their unsavory taste; as may appear by this, that a woman said to her neighbor, 'Alas, gossip, what shall we now do at church, since all the saints are taken away; since all the goodly sights we were wont to have are gone; since we cannot hear the like piping, singing, chaunting, and playing upon the organs that we could before!' But, dearly beloved, we ought greatly to rejoice and give God thanks that our churches are delivered out of all those things which displeased God so sore and filthily defiled his holy house and his place of prayer."

The thirty-two godly and learned commissioners appointed by King Edward VI. to reform ecclesiastical laws and observances submitted the following advice: [1] "In reading chapters and singing psalms, ministers and clergymen must think of this diligently, that God is not only to be praised by them, but that others are to be brought to perform the same worship by their counsel and example. Wherefore, let them pronounce their words distinctly, and let their singing be clear and easy, that everything may be understood by the auditors. So that 'tis our pleasure, that the quavering operose music which is called *figured* should be wholly laid aside,[2] since it often makes such a noise in the ears of the people that they cannot understand what is said." "Certainly," says Ames in answer to the taunts of Dr. Burgess, "these were neither distracted nor stupid men; whence their prejudice came, let the Rejoinder himself judge."[3]

"In the English Convocation, held in the year 1562, in Queen Elizabeth's time, for settling the Liturgy, the retaining of the custom of kneeling at the sacrament, of the cross in baptism, and of organs, carried only by the casting vote."[4] Hetherington's account of the matter is as follows:[5] "In the beginning of the year 1562, a meeting of the Convocation was held, in which the subject of further reformation was vigorously discussed on both sides . . . [Among the alterations proposed was this]: 'That the use of organs be laid aside.' When the vote came to be taken, on these propositions, forty-three

---

[1] *Reform. Leg. de Dir. Offic.*, Cap. v.
[2] "*Vibratam illam et operosam musicam, quæ figurata dicitur, auferri placet.*"
[3] *Church Cerem.*, p. 406.
[4] *Dr. Henry's Hist., Strype's Annals*, p. 363.
[5] *Hist. Westminster Assembly*, p. 30.

voted for them and thirty-five against; but when the proxies were counted, the balance was turned; the final state of the vote being fifty-eight for and fifty-nine against. Thus it was determined by a single vote, and that the proxy of an absent person who did not hear the reasoning that the Prayer-Book should remain unimproved, that there should be no further reformation, that there should be no relief granted to those whose consciences felt aggrieved by the admixture of human inventions in the worship of God."

In 1564, during Queen Elizabeth's reign, considerable discussion was had touching the use of vestments in public worship. Bishop Horn wrote to Gualter at Zurich about the matter. He and Bullinger replied to him recommending moderation. Whereupon Samson and Humphrey, in February, 1565, wrote to the Zurich divines giving "a copious account of the grounds on which they founded their refusal to obey" the orders of the Queen and Parliament. Bullinger answered them by again recommending moderation.[1] This letter of Bullinger to Samson and Humphrey was sent to Horn and Grindal, who published it. "Upon this Samson and Humphrey wrote to Zurich complaining of the printing their letter, and carried their complaints much further than to the matter of the vestments: they complained of the music and organs, of making sponsors in baptism answer in the child's name, of the Court of Faculties, and the praying for dispensations."[2]

---

[1] One is here reminded of Luther's words: "Too much discretion is displeasing to God."

[2] The author of *Primitive Truth*, citing Bp. Burnet, *Reformation*, Vol. iii., pp. 308-310.

These facts are sufficient to show that the Church of England was at one time on the verge of eliminating instrumental music along with other relics of Popery from her public services; and had she been thoroughly reformed in accordance with the wishes of her purest divines she would have conformed her practice, in this matter, to that of the Reformed churches on the continent. But the taste and the will of an arbitrary female head of the church determined her usages in a contrary direction. The history deserves to be pondered most seriously.

What were the views of the English Puritans on this subject has already been indicated when the question was under consideration in regard to the position assumed concerning it by the Westminster Assembly of Divines. It is not necessary to exhibit their sentiments by further appeals to authority. To their almost unanimous opposition to instrumental music in the public worship of the church, as unscriptural and Popish, there were some exceptions, among whom was the justly celebrated Richard Baxter, a great man, but neither a great Calvinist nor a great Presbyterian. Those who wish to see his arguments in favor of a temperate employment of instrumental music in church-worship can find them in the fifth volume of his works, edited by Orme, page 499: arguments about as weak as those by which he attempted to support the Grotian theory of the atonement. As they may, to some extent, be considered in the examination of the arguments in favor of instrumental music, they will not be noticed in this place. I cannot pass from this reference to the English Puritans without pausing to express the conviction that, whatever may have been some of their peculiar characteristics—and even these have been magnified and caricatured by opponents who were partly or wholly destitute of their religious earnestness—no purer exponents of the truth of God as set forth in the Holy Scriptures have existed on earth since the days of the apostles; and the growing defection from the views they maintained touching the purity of worship, which now conspicuously marks the English-speaking non-prelatic churches, carries in it the ominous symptoms of apostasy from the gospel. Some few yet stand firm against what is now called, in a painfully significant phrase, the "down-grade" tendencies of this age. Prominent among them is that eminent servant of Christ —a star in his right hand—the Rev. Charles H. Spurgeon, who not only proclaims with power the pure doctrines of God's Word, but retains and upholds an apostolic simplicity of worship. The great congregation which is blessed with the privilege of listening to his instructions has no organ "to assist" them in singing their praises to their God and Saviour. They find their vocal organs sufficient. Their tongues and voices express the gratitude of their hearts.

It is almost needless to cite the example of the Church of Scotland. She was—with the exception of an unholy alliance between the church and the state, a baneful source of incalculable evils, "a spring of woes unnumbered," to the former—a glorious instance of a church as completely reformed as could be expected in this present, imperfect, pre-millennial condition. Even the permissive liturgy of John Knox she soon threw off as a swathing band from her free limbs, and for centuries she knew nothing of instrumental music in her public services. Would that she now retained this primitive purity of worship! But within a half-century back, in consequence of the agitation persistently pursued by some who clamored for a more artistic "celebration" of worship, the Established Church relaxed its testimony, and consented to make the question of instrumental music an "open" one—that is, the matter was left to the option of individual congregations. Meanwhile the Free Church stood firm, and has so stood until recently. Dr. Begg, in his work on organs, could express his gratitude for the conservative attitude of his church on the subject, and Dr. Candlish deprecated the discussion of the question as fraught with peril. But they have fallen asleep, and the church of their love is now, by the action of her Presbyteries, making it an "open question." The floodgates are up, and the result is by no means uncertain: the experience of the American Presbyterian Church will be that of the Scottish.

The Irish Presbyterian Church has for years seriously debated the question in her General Assembly. So far she has refused to make it an open one; but the pressure of a heavy minority, it may almost with certainty be expected, will prevail in breaking through the dykes of scriptural conservatism. The fact, however, that to the present hour that noble church maintains its opposition to instrumental music contributes no unimportant element to the historical argument against its use. It is likely that the question has never been subjected to so thorough-going an examination as it has met in the protracted discussions of her supreme court. She is now almost the last great witness for the simple singing of praise in public worship. Should the standard of her testimony go down, it must be left to small, seceded bodies, or to individuals, to continue the witness-bearing and the contest for a simplicity of worship from which the majority in the church have apostatized.

The non-prelatic churches, Independent and Presbyterian, began their development on the American continent without instrumental music. They followed the English Puritans and the Scottish Church, which had adopted the principles of the Calvinistic Reformed Church. How the organ came to be gradually introduced into them it were bootless to inquire. They began right, but have more and more departed from the simple genius of Christian worship. On what grounds they have done this it would be well for them to stop and inquire. For if there be any force in argument, their present position cannot be maintained. It is a clear departure from the practice of the church, both early and reformed. The United Presbyterian Church has but recently given way. A respectable minority opposes the defection, but what the issue will be events do not yet furnish sufficient data to determine. The Associate Reformed Church has not yet receded from the pure principles and practice of their forefathers. May God grant them grace to continue in their maintenance! The time may ere long come when those who stand on these principles and refuse to yield to the demands of a latitudinarian age will be attracted by adherence to a common sentiment towards a formal union with each other. It may be made a question whether the retention of a pure gospel-worship does not constitute a reason for the existence of a distinctive organization.

It has thus been proved, by an appeal to historical facts, that the church, although lapsing more and more into defection from the truth and into a corruption of apostolic practice, had no instrumental music for twelve hundred years; and that the Calvinistic Reformed Church ejected it from its services as an element of Popery, even the Church of England having come very nigh to its extrusion from her worship. The historical argument, therefore, combines with the scriptural and the confessional to raise a solemn and powerful protest against its employment by the Presbyterian Church. It is heresy in the sphere of worship.

VI.

ARGUMENTS IN FAVOR OF INSTRUMENTAL MUSIC CONSIDERED.

IN the preceding argument the appeal has been taken to the Scriptures and to the Presbyterian standards as interpreting them; and historical proofs of the practice of the church have, in addition, been presented chiefly for the purpose of showing what was the usage of the apostles and of the churches which they organized. Any arguments produced in favor of instrumental music in the public worship of the church must profess to be grounded in the same considerations—that is, they must assume to be derived from the same sources as those from which the foregoing proofs have been sought, or they are to be regarded as unworthy of answers. Those founded upon human taste or wisdom trifle with the gravity of the subject. They refer to a standard which can have no possible authority in a question which concerns the public worship of God. Such are the common arguments, for example, that instrumental music assists devotion, that it stimulates and exalts religious feeling, and that it imparts dignity, grace and attractiveness to the services of the church. They are all based upon expediency, and are therefore irrelevant to the consideration of a question which can only be legitimately decided by the expressed authority of God. There is no middle ground between submission to God's revealed will and a worship dictated by the fancies of sinners. Only two sorts of argument consequently, will now be examined:

1. Those which profess to be derived immediately from the Scriptures.

(1.) It is urged that God himself has sanctioned the use of instrumental music in public worship, and the Scriptures are pleaded in proof of this assertion. Surely what God has approved must be right; it cannot be condemned by man. The fallacy here consists in the affirmation that what God approved at a certain place, at a certain time, and in certain circumstances, he approves at all places, at all times, and in all circumstances. It is forgotten that there is a distinction between moral laws founded in the eternal nature of God, which are immutable, and positive enactments grounded in the special determinations of his will, which may be changed at his pleasure. He gave to Adam permission to eat of the tree of life in Paradise; he revoked it when he fell. He commanded his people in the old dispensation to observe circumcision and the passover; he has in the new changed that enactment, and commands them to observe baptism and the Lord's supper. He once commanded them to offer bloody sacrifices, and to observe other special rites at the temple; he now commands them to refrain from what were at that time binding duties. And even during the time when it was obligatory to offer sacrificial and typical worship at a certain place—the temple, he forbade them to present it at another place—the synagogue. In like manner, there was a time when he positively commanded the use of instrumental music at the temple and prohibited its use in the synagogue; and since the temple with its distinctive services has passed away, he forbids the employment of it now in any place. God approved circumcision, the passover, the offering of sacrifice, meat offerings, drink offerings, ablutions, and the like. Therefore he approves them at all times, and approves them now. Such is the logic of the argument under consideration. Will the Christian now circumcise his children, eat the passover, offer sacrifices, bloody and unbloody, and employ ablutions in his worship? Why not? Did not God once approve them? The reed pierces the hand that leans upon it. The argument proves too much, and is in many respects confessed to be worthless. God did once approve instrumental music. Granted; but does that show that he approves it now? On the contrary, he condemns it now. It was one of those positive enactments which he has been pleased to change. It may be replied, that when he has willed the disuse of an ancient ordinance, he has substituted another in its place; baptism, for instance, in the room of circumcision, and the Lord's supper in lieu of the passover; but the same does not hold in regard to instrumental music. But, in the first place, this is not universally true. What has he substituted for sacrificial worship? In the second place, he has substituted simple singing in the place of singing with the accompaniment of instruments. In a word, God once approved the whole ritual of the temple. He disapproves it now; and he who would introduce any part of it into the Christian church turns Jew and revolts from Christ to Moses. This is true of instrumental music, as has been already proved.

(2.) Instrumental music is not condemned or prohibited in the New Testament Scriptures. This position could be consistently taken only by a Prelatist of the Ritualistic school, who contends that the church is clothed with a discretionary power to decree rites and ceremonies; and we have seen that even the Convocation of the English Church that adopted the Thirty-nine Articles did not incorporate into them such a principle. To those who cherish a respect for the doctrines of the Reformed Church, of the English Puritans, and of the Church of Scotland the principle is of cardinal value, that whatsoever is not commanded, either explicitly or implicitly, in the New Testament Scriptures is forbidden to the New Testament church. It is enough to them that those Scriptures are silent concerning any practice, to secure its exclusion from the services of the church. It has at the outset of this discussion been shown, that under the Old Testament dispensation a divine warrant was necessary to the introduction of any element into the public worship of God's house. Every thing was shut out in respect to which it could be said that God "commanded it not;" and in those instances in which his silence was taken advantage of to inject into his worship what the will or wisdom of man dictated, his anger smoked against the invader of his prerogative. What proof is there that the same principle does not prevail in the new dispensation? The New Testament closes with the prohibitory statute, enforced in the Old Testament Scriptures, against adding to or taking from the words of God. Nothing is left to human discretion but those natural circumstances which condition the actions of all human societies. The Scriptures are sufficient for all the wants of the church.

Their prescriptions thoroughly furnish the man of God for all good works. He who advocates the infusion into the worship of the church of what God has not authorized takes the ground that the Scriptures are not sufficient, and that human wisdom is entitled to supplement its defects; he claims to be wiser than the Head of the church himself.

Instrumental music is prohibited by the absence of any warrant in the New Testament for its use; it is prohibited by the declaration that the temple-worship, with all its peculiar appurtenances, is abolished; it is prohibited by the fact that it is not included in the inspired enumeration of the elements of public worship; and it is prohibited by the practice of the apostles, which must be deemed regulative of the customs of the church by all who revere the authority of inspiration.

(3.) Instrumental music is justified in the church on earth by the consideration that it is represented as employed in the church in heaven. Are we not to be heavenly-minded? Whether the language of the Apocalyptic seer is to be interpreted literally or not, whether harpers will harp on real harps in heaven or not, it is not material to the present purpose to determine. If it be admitted that instrumental music will be employed in heaven, this argument will not be helped. It would be invalid, because it would prove too much. All that the glorified saints will experience in heaven cannot, from the nature of the case, be realized on earth. They will not need to confess and deplore continually recurring sins, but we are obliged to do so below. They will sing, but they will hardly chant in mournful strains;

> "Show pity, Lord, O Lord, forgive,
>   Let a repenting rebel live;
>   Are not thy mercies large and free,
>   May not a sinner trust in thee?
>
> "Should sudden vengeance seize my breath,
>   I must pronounce thee just in death;
>   And if my soul were sent to hell,
>   Thy righteous law approves it well."

Thus we sing, however, till our dying breath. One of the holiest ministers I ever knew, at ninety-three years of age, on the verge of his translation to glory, wrote that he was constrained to sing those penitential words. It is not likely that they wet the sacramental bread with the tears of penitence, but this we do while we obey the injunction of our Lord, "Do this in remembrance of me." They neither marry nor are given in marriage, but it would scarcely be legitimate for us to argue from their example to what our practice should be. If we did, the church on earth would be, as Owen says, in the condition of the kingdom of the Romans when it consisted only of men, "it had like to have been the matter of a single generation." They cannot be conceived as beseeching sinners to be reconciled to God, but we, should we imitate them in this regard, would ill discharge our duty to the unconverted souls around us. But enough. It is plain that the argument proves too much, and is, therefore, nothing worth. It tries to prove from the heavenly world what we have seen some endeavoring to prove from the Jewish temple. Both arguments burst from their own plethora. If God had commanded us to do what is done in heaven, we might make the effort to obey, whatever might be the success or failure attending it; but until such a command can be produced, we are not warranted to turn harpers and harp upon harps in the church on earth.

(4.) The use of instrumental music in the church is justified upon the scriptural principle that we ought to consecrate every talent we possess to the service of God. This argument is also futile, because it proves too much. It would prove that the sculptor should install his statues in the sanctuary, that the painter should hang his pictures upon its walls, that the mechanic should contribute the products of his skill as "object-lessons" for the elucidation of gospel truths, and that the architect should, by massive piles, express the greatness of God, and by the multiplicity of their minute details the manifoldness of his works. Avaunt! The argument is suited only to a Papist.

(5.) Instrumental music is among the *Adiaphora*— the things indifferent. The law of liberty entitles us to its use. The answer is easy. That law exempts us, in things sacred, from obedience to the commandments of men, and, so far as our individual consciences are concerned, from compliance with their scruples and crotchets. But it cannot free us from the obligation to obey God. Now, God commanded the Jews to use instrumental music at the temple, and did not command them to employ it in the tabernacle for most part of its existence, or in the synagogue. They obeyed him in both respects. It is manifest that it was not a thing indifferent with them. Neither is it with Christians. The truth is, that it is an abuse of language to rank among things indifferent any concomitant of public worship which becomes a part and parcel of it. On the contrary, it has in these remarks been shown that, so far from being in that category, there is nothing about which the living God expresses so vehement a jealousy as the method in which men approach him in worship. Indifferent? Nadab and Abihu thought so, but they made a dreadful mistake.

But if instrumental music is regarded as a thing indifferent, it is conceded that it is not necessary; it may or may not be used; it is not required by duty. Here, then, the law of charity comes in, and challenges obedience. It is, of course, admitted that, on the supposition, the liberty of the individual is not bound, so far as his views and his private acts are involved, but his practice, in the presence of brethren whom he may deem weak, is bound by the law of charity. Is not this the principle asserted by the inspired apostle in regard to the eating of meat offered to idols? He affirmed the liberty of the believer to eat of it. But the law of individual liberty was checked by the weaker conscience of his brother, to which the law of charity required that respect be shown. Paul maintained his perfect right to eat, but declared: "If meat make my brother to offend, I will eat no flesh while the world standeth, lest I make my brother to offend." His private liberty was, in the presence of a weak brother, not only restrained, but controlled by the higher law of love. If, therefore, a believer chooses to regale himself with the melody or harmony of instruments, he is not bound; but if instrumental music in public worship stumbles the consciences of brethren, regarded, though they may be, as entertaining groundless scruples about it, as, confessedly, it is not a matter of obligation, should not the law of charity lead its advocates to say: "If instrumental music in public worship make our brethren to offend, we will not employ it while the world standeth, lest we make our brethren to offend." There are those who, when they hear it, pray that God will not hold them responsible for its use in his sanctuary. They are sincere; and if it be a thing indifferent, why should it not, for their sake, be discarded? The law of brotherly charity asks, Why? That law certainly takes precedence of the liberty to gratify taste, and its infraction cannot be unattended with guilt.

2. Arguments derived from the Confession of Faith:

(1.) It is not claimed, so far as I know, by the advocates of instrumental music that it is necessary to any performance at all of the act of singing praise, but it is claimed that it is necessary to the "decent and orderly" performance of that act. It is justified by an appeal to the last clause of the following sentence of the Confession of Faith, about which so much has been said in the course of the foregoing argument: "There are some circumstances concerning the worship of God and government of the church, common to human actions and societies, which are to be ordered by the light of nature and Christian prudence, *according to the general rules of the Word, which are always to be observed.*"[1] Among those general rules of the Word cited in the proof-texts, supporting this whole statement, beginning, "there are some circumstances," is the following: "Let all things be done decently and in order." This, it is claimed, warrants the use of instrumental music. Among the "all things" to "be done decently and in

---

[1] Chap. i., Sec. vi.

order" is the singing of praise, and instrumental music is necessary to this thing being "done decently and in order."

First, It must be observed that the last clause of the statement of the Confession, the clause which is used in this argument for instrumental music, has reference to the "circumstances" mentioned in that statement. It is these circumstances, and not something else different from them, in regard to which "the general rules of the Word," including this one, "Let all things be done decently and in order," "are always to be observed." Now it has already been clearly pointed out that these circumstances are circumstances "common to human actions and societies." It is precisely such circumstances concerning which the statement of the Confession enjoins that they be ordered according to the general rules of the Word. It is precisely such circumstances, consequently, that that statement requires to "be done decently and in order." The question before us, then, is this: Is instrumental music one of those circumstances? It has, in a previous part of this discussion, by a somewhat pains-taking argument, been proved that it cannot be one of them. Those circumstances have been shown to be undistinctive conditions upon which the actions of all societies are performed. They are common to them all. But instrumental music is not common to the actions of all societies. It cannot, therefore, be one of the circumstances indicated by the statement in the Confession. The conclusion is irresistible that; so far as that statement is concerned, it is not necessary to the decent and orderly performance of the singing of praise as a part of church-worship. This particular argument in favor of instrumental music will be still further considered as the discussion draws towards its close.

Secondly, The argument takes on the aspect of preposterous arrogance, as containing an indictment of the true church of God in almost all the centuries of the Christian era for an indecent and disorderly singing of praise in its public worship, not to speak of the church in the old dispensation in its ordinary Sabbath-day services. It would be folly to test the question of the decent and orderly, or the indecorous and disorderly, singing of praise by a temporary standard, especially one erected in a modern and corrupt condition of the nominal church. Shall the standard by which the practice of the Christian church—leaving out of account the Jewish—for twelve centuries is to be judged be one in which the Church of Rome slowly and reluctantly acquiesced as late as the middle or the close of the thirteenth century? And by this standard will we convict of indecorous and disorderly worship the Reformed churches of Europe, the Swiss, the French and the Dutch, the churches of Scotland for centuries, the English Puritans and the Presbyterian Church of Ireland? Has it been left to the church in these latter days to discover the only decorous and orderly way in which God's praises shall be sung? The supposition is intolerable.

The same considerations avail against the plea that instrumental music is a help in the singing of praise. If the church of Christ has not felt the need of this help during the greater part of its existence, it requires no argument to show that she can do without it now. It

ARGUMENTS FOR INSTRUMENTAL MUSIC. 191

may be admitted that it is a help to such "rendering" (!) of singing as is demanded by ears cultivated for the enjoyment of Italian operas and the like artistic performances. But that is quite a different thing from admitting that it is a help to the singing of praise by humble and penitent sinners, by the afflicted people of God passing as cross-bearing pilgrims through a world to which they are crucified and which is crucified to them. The discussion is gratuitous and needless. It is sufficient to say, that that cannot be a true help to worship which the Being to be worshipped does not himself approve.

(2.) It is contended that instrumental music is to be ranked among the circumstances allowed by the Confession of Faith, and that this is proved by the fact that it is on the same foot as other circumstances about which there is no dispute: such as houses of worship, reading sermons, the length of sermons, of prayers and of singing, bells, tuning-forks and pitch-pipes, tune-books, and the like.

One would be entitled to meet this argument upon the general ground already so often and earnestly maintained, that all the circumstances remitted by the Confession to the discretion—the natural judgment—of the church are common to human actions and societies, and are such as belong to the natural sphere in which the acts of all societies are performed, and, therefore, cannot be distinctively spiritual or even ecclesiastical. As instrumental music, used in professedly spiritual and actually ecclesiastical worship, cannot possibly be assigned to that category, it is for that patent reason ruled out by the very terms of the Confession's statement.

This ground I hold to be impregnable. But inasmuch as it is a fact that certain minds do consider instrumental music as saveable to the church for the reason that it may be viewed as standing on the same foot with the circumstances which have been mentioned, I will endeavor to meet their difficulties, albeit at the conscious expense of strict logical consistency, by following this argument into its minute details; and I pray that the Spirit of God may bestow his guidance in this last step of the discussion.

First, It has been argued, that the use of instrumental music is a circumstance of the same kind with the building of a house of worship and the selection of its arrangements; that it is not an absolutely necessary condition of the church's acts that it should hold its meetings in edifices: they might be held, as has often in fact been done, in the open air. To this the obvious reply is, that this circumstance is one common to the acts of all societies. They must meet somewhere, and it is of course competent to all of them to determine, whether they shall be subjected to the inconveniences of open-air assemblages, or avail themselves of the advantages afforded by buildings. So of the arrangements and furniture of the edifices in which they convene. Every society, even an infidel society, has this circumstance conditioning its meetings and acts, either as necessary to any performance of them or as necessary to their decorous and orderly discharge. But instrumental music is not such a circumstance: it is not common to human actions and societies. This destroys the alleged analogy, and consequently the argument founded upon it fails.

Secondly, The same disproof is applicable to the assumed analogy between the alleged circumstance of instrumental music and that of reading sermons. It is urged that a sermon must be delivered in one of two ways: either with or without reading, and there is discretion left to the church to elect between them. If she thinks reading the better way, she is at liberty to employ it. So with the choice of instrumental music as a mode in which praise shall be sung. There might be, as there has been, some discussion in regard to the legitimacy of reading sermons. But that question aside, and the argument being considered on its own ground, it is sufficient to reply that the analogy asserted does not obtain. The delivery of discourses, speeches, reports and resolutions is an act common to all human societies. Now, it is competent to all societies to say whether they shall be simply spoken or read, whether the delivery shall be extemporaneous or from manuscript. They can, each for itself, determine the circumstance of the mode in which an act common to all shall be performed. But the singing of praise in the worship of God is not an act common to all societies. It is therefore not one in regard to which the Confession grants the liberty to the church of fixing the circumstance of the mode in which it shall be done.[1]

Thirdly, The same line of argument, it is contended, holds good with reference to the discretionary power of the church to order the circumstances of the length of

---

[1] In addition to this, let it be noticed that in preaching to men worship is not directly offered to God; in singing praise it is, at least in great part.

sermons, of prayers, and of singing. But, it is replied, all societies must, of necessity, fix the time allotted to their several exercises, or their meetings would be failures. Nature itself dictates this. The church, therefore, has the natural right to order this circumstance in connection with all her services. But the question o determining the length of an exercise is a very different one from that of introducing the exercise at all. There is no analogy between the determination of the time to be allowed to all acts, and the determination of the legitimacy of some special act. The adjustment of the length of its exercises is a circumstance common to all societies. The employment of instrumental music, as a concomitant of worship, is a circumstance peculiar to the church as a distinctive society. The analogy in every respect breaks down.

Fourthly, If the church has bells, it is asked, why may it not have organs? They are both instruments of sound which serve an ecclesiastical purpose. The answer is so obvious that one feels almost ashamed to give it. The bell is not directly connected with worship; the organ is. The bell stops ringing before the worship begins, the organ accompanies the worship itself. There is not the least likeness between them, so far as this question is concerned. A bell simply marks the time for assembling. So does a clock; and we may as well institute a comparison between the hands of the clock at a certain hour and instrumenta music in worship after that hour, as between the sound of the bell and it. The question is in regard to a concomitant of worship, not as to something that precedes it and gives way to it.

Fifthly, It is by some gravely contended that if tuning-forks and pitch-pipes may be used, so may organs. The same answer as was returned to the immediately foregoing argument is pertinent here. Did those who submit this argument ever notice the use made of a tuning-fork or a pitch-pipe by a leader of singing? It is struck or sounded in a way to be heard by the leader himself, and when by means of it he has got the pitch of the tune to be sung, it is put into his pocket, where it snugly and silently rests while the singing proceeds. It no more accompanies the worship than does a bell. Like it, it stops sounding before the act of worship begins. What analogy is there between it and an instrument that accompanies every note of the singing by a corresponding note of its own. Assign to the organ the same office as the humbler tuning-fork or pitch-pipe, namely, merely to give the leader of the simple singing the pitch of the tunes, and who would object to it? The question of organs would be as quiet as they would be. One toot before the singing, and then they would be, what they ought to be during the public singing of praise, as silent as the grave. One cannot help wondering that the admirers of this "majestic instrument" would employ a comparison which reduces it to a pitch so low!

Sixthly, There is only one other argument of this minute class which will be considered. It is one which I have known some brethren to maintain as men do a last redoubt. It is argued that instrumental music is just as fairly entitled to rank among the circumstances indicated by the Confession of Faith as is a tune-book.

Does a tune-book assist the singing of praise? So does an organ. If the church has discretion in employing one kind of assistance to singing, why not another?

Has it not occurred to the minds of those who insist so strenuously upon this view that they may be using a tune-book to accomplish an office to which it may be inadequate, when they wield it to knock down arguments derived from the Old Testament and the New Testament Scriptures, from the old dispensation and the new, from the practice of the Jewish synagogue, of the apostles, of the whole church for twelve hundred years, and of the Calvinistic Reformed Church for centuries? Does it not occur to them also that there may be a flaw in the statement of their argument? Expanded, it is this: Whatever *assists* the singing of praise is a legitimate circumstance; the tune-book and the organ alike assist, etc., therefore they are alike legitimate circumstances. The true statement would be, whatever is *necessary* to the singing of praise is a legitimate circumstance; the tune-book and the organ are alike so necessary; therefore they are alike legitimate circumstances. It behooves them to show that the organ is necessary to the singing of praise. It is not enough to say that it assists it. They cannot prove its necessity. Praise has been and is sung without the organ. But it also behooves me to show that the tune-book is necessary to the singing of praise, that it is a condition without which it could not be done. If this can be evinced, as the organ is not necessary to singing, it does not, as is assumed, stand on the same foot with the tune-book, and the argument is unfounded.

It will be granted that a tune is necessary to modulated singing—that is, to singing which is not merely the prolongation of a single note, and that could not be denominated singing. But the tune-book gives the tune. The tune is necessary to singing; the tune-book is necessary to the tune; therefore the tune-book is necessary to singing. Need this simple argument be pressed? Whence the tune, if not from the tune-book? Is it improvised by the leading singer? Suppose that it may be, and he would be the only singer. It would be impossible for others to unite with him.

It may be replied that the organ also gives the tune. This is a mistake. The organ is as much indebted to the tune-book for the tune as is a leading singer. If the organist should improvise the tune, where would be the singing? It will hardly be contended that a solo on the organ would be the singing of the congregation, or that the organ sings at all.

It may still be said that the tune-book is not necessary to singing, since it is a fact that singing is often done without it. This is a mistake also. The tune-book may be absent as a book, but the tune it contains is present in the mind of the leading singer. He remembers what he got from it. It is a necessity to him, whether literally absent or present. He cannot sing without the tune, and the tune is in the tune-book.

Finally, the mighty contest may yet be maintained on the ground that some leading singers do not know the musical notes, and, therefore, cannot depend on the tune-book for the tune. True, there are some who are ignorant of the notes, but all the same they depend on the tune-book, not immediately, but mediately and really. For the tune is learned, in the first instance, only from some one who does know the notes and got the tune from the book. The tune-book is the first cause of the tune, and is necessary to its existence. Of course, tunes are learned by the ear. Most members of a congregation so learn them. But these persons acquire them from the leading singer, and he received them from the tune-book. So that, look at the matter as we may, the tune-book is necessary to the singing of praise: it conditions its performance.

If, now, it be objected that the tune-book is a circumstance not common to human actions and societies, and is equally, with instrumental music, according to this argument, excluded from the discretionary control of the church, I answer, That is true. It is circumstances in the natural sphere, those which attend actions as actions, and not this or that particular action of a distinctive society, that fall within the discretion of the church. Consequently both of these circumstances—the tune-book and instrumental music—fall without that discretion. They both condition the performance of an act peculiar to the church. But the difference between them is this: One is necessary to the performance of a commanded duty, namely, the singing of praise, and the other is not. The singing of praise is undoubtedly a commanded duty, and it follows that what is a necessary condition of its discharge comes also under the scope of command. It is, therefore, not discretionary with the church to employ it; it is obligatory. It must be employed, or the commanded duty fails to be done. It is not so with instrumental music. It is not a condition necessary to the commanded duty of singing praise; neither is it a natural circumstance conditioning the acts of all societies. It is, therefore, neither obligatory upon nor discretionary with the church to use it. It is consequently excluded.

VII.

Concluding Remarks.

The foregoing argument has proceeded principally by two steps. The first is: Whatsoever, in connection with the public worship of the church, is not commanded by Christ, either expressly or by good and necessary consequence, in his Word, is forbidden. The second is: Instrumental music, in connection with the public worship of the church is not so commanded by Christ. The conclusion is: Instrumental music, in connection with the public worship of the church, is forbidden. If the premises are materially true, and if they are logically connected in the argument, the conclusion is irresistible. The first premise, which is denied by Romanists, Prelatists, and Latitudinarians, has been established by proofs derived from the Scriptures. The position that the church has power to decree rites connected with the worship of God's house, rites not prescribed in the divine Word, is confessedly a doctrine of men, making a substantive addition to the only sufficient, complete and infallible rule of faith and practice. Of those who contend for this principle, the Romanist alone is consistent. It is plain that such a discretionary power in the church could only be grounded in her possession of continued inspiration. If she have that gift her authority is equal to that of the inspired organizers and instructors of the church themselves. She can supplement the Scriptures. But the claim to inspiration can only be substantiated by the working of miracles. This Rome admits, and meets the requirement by appealing to *her* miracles. These professed miracles are, however, of such a character as not to be placed above impeachment. They may be accounted for upon natural principles. They never rise to the point of creative power, nor of the power that restores life to the dead. The Protestant church, therefore, rejects the claim of Rome to inspiration, and infallibility, and is consequently bound to deny the authority of that church, or any other, to decree rites and ceremonies not prescribed in the Word of God. For a church theoretically to make such a claim is to confess itself, to that extent, apostate. It is in flagrant rebellion against the sole authority of Christ as expressed in his Word. The past history of the church is a comment upon the correctness of this indictment.

The second premise, namely, that instrumental music is, in connection with the public worship of the church, not commanded by Christ, either expressly or by good and necessary consequence in his Word, is acknowledged to be true by all consistent Presbyterians. One would, therefore, argue that they would exclude it from the public worship of the church; and so, indeed, they have done until a comparatively recent period. On that very ground they have justly refused to employ it. How is the amazing change to its employment to be accounted for? How is it that in Scotland such a revolution against the historic position of the Presbyterian Church is now in full progress? How is it that in the conservative Scotch-Irish Church so formidable an effort is making to upset its testimony and its practice in relation to this subject? How is it that such men as Breckinridge and Thornwell, in the American Presbyterian Church, were hardly cold in their graves before, in the very places where they had thundered forth their contentions for the mighty principle which demands a divine warrant for every element of doctrine, government and worship, and where they had, in obedience to that principle, utterly refused to admit instrumental music into the church, the organ pealed forth its triumphs over their views? How is this state of things to be explained?

There is a class who look with indifference upon the question, who are willing that human opinions shall prevail and human tastes shall be gratified in the arrangements of public worship. It is needless to say that, as they disregard alike the teachings of God's Word and the testimonies of their forefathers, they are countenancing a course which must, if not interrupted by the extraordinary interposition of divine providence or divine grace, land the church in open apostasy from the gospel.

There is a second class who maintain the prelatical theory, that whatsoever is not expressly—that is, in explicit terms—forbidden in the New Testament Scriptures is permitted. Those who hold this view break with the Westminster standards, play into the hands of Ritualists, and convert the ordinances of the Presbyterian Church, as the maintainers of the same principle have those of the Anglican, into propædeutics for the *cultus* of Rome.

There is a third class who hold that, as instrumental music was commanded of God in the Old Testament church, it is justifiable in that of the New Testament. It is one of the things which God himself has prescribed. This is very extraordinary ground for Christians to take. It is hard to believe that they would contend for the following positions, logically validated by their view: That every positive enactment of the divine will under the old dispensation passes over unchanged in its authority to the new; that the Christian church is the Jewish temple, or even modelled in conformity with it; that the types of the Old Testament are continued in the new; that what was not warrantable to the Jew in the worship of the synagogue is justifiable to the Christian in that of the church; that all the external elements of worship authorized in the Psalms are allowable in the Christian church, for, upon that ground, animal sacrifices would also be proper; and that the whole nominal church, from the apostles to Thomas Aquinas, in 1250, was mistaken in regard to this matter. Still, carrying with it these consequences as it does, this view is supported by some in the Presbyterian Church.

There is a fourth class—and it is believed to be the largest—who hold theoretically to the great principle, that whatsoever is not commanded is forbidden, but deny its applicability to instrumental music in connection with the public worship of the church. They contend that it is one of the circumstances which the Confession of Faith assigns to the discretionary control of the church. This is probably the chief explanation of the wonderful change that is passing over the Presbyterian Church in the sphere of worship. It is to be feared that very few of her ministers and ruling elders have ever thoroughly studied the *Doctrine of Circumstances*. How many of them have ever expounded it to the people over whom the Holy Ghost has made them overseers? Nothing is more common than to hear it said that this question is one concerning a "circumstantial detail" of subordinate value, and that the issue, as one of minor importance, must give way to others of more commanding interest which are pressing upon the church. This confusion of thought would be surprising were it not so general. What a profound mistake is couched in such remarks! Instead of the circumstances relegated by the Confession to the discretion of the church being circumstantial details of worship, they are not details of worship at all. Instead of their being of secondary importance, they are indispensable— not as parts of worship, but as natural conditions of its performance. Without them there would be, there could be, no joint worship. The assemblies of the saints would be a dream.

The change which is taking place more and more in the worship of the Presbyterian Church is due to the combined influence of the views held by all these classes, but the chief peril results from that maintained by the last which has been named. It is almost inconceivable that the majority of the officers and members of the Presbyterian Church can have abandoned the consecrated principle that a divine warrant is needed for every element which enters into the worship of God's house. Were that so, open apostasy in the department of worship would be acknowledged. But of what avail is the professed acceptance of the principle, if its application be refused? How it happens that this principle, which was construed by the Presbyterian reformers and the framers of the Westminster standards as excluding instrumental music from public worship, and was so applied by the Presbyterian Church almost universally for centuries after the Reformation, is now interpreted in such a way as to admit this Popish innovation into the once simple and evangelical services of that church, defies comprehension except upon one supposition. It is, that the Presbyterian Church is slackening her grasp upon her ancient testimonies, broadening her practice in conformity with the demands of worldly taste, and is therefore more and more treading the path of defection from the scriptural principles which she professes. The revolution in her practice began in the American Church scarcely beyond the recollection of some now living, and certainly in the Scottish Churches within that of those who are not yet fifty years of age. But once begun, what rapid progress it made! What would Gillespie and Calderwood now say, what Chalmers and Candlish, Cunningham and Begg, what Mason, Breckinridge and Thornwell—what would they say, were they permitted to rise from their graves, and revisit the scenes of their labors —the churches for which they toiled and prayed?

It is evident that a great change has taken place. Now, either it has been for the better or for the worse. If it be contended that it is for the better, these great men, and thousands who thought as they did, are pronounced to have been ignorant of the Scriptures and the principles of the Presbyterian system. Who are they that will assume such a censorship? Let them by argument prove their claim to this arrogated superiority. If they cannot—and they certainly have not yet done it—let them abandon the unwarrantable attempt to revolutionize the long-standing and scriptural practice of their church, and, ere it be too late, return to the good old paths trodden by their fathers. We are not bound to wear the yoke of human authority, it will be said. No. But these men wore the yoke of divine authority, and we ought to do the same. This is your own human assertion, it will be replied. Yes. But it is an assertion proved by irrefragable argument, founded on the Scriptures, the Presbyterian standards and the history of the true Church of Christ. The burden of proof rests upon those who have made, or who countenance, this change. They offer proof derived from the principles of nature and from human taste. What argument from Scripture is presented is such as would make us turn Jews and worship at the temple. It would not even convert us into Jews who worshipped at the synagogue. It is an argument which would take the Christian church over the ruins of the synagogue back to the temple, and in effect re-enact the madness of Julian by an attempt to construct again that abrogated institute.

But whatever may be the want of satisfactory argument to ground this wide-spread and astounding defection from the old, conservative position of the Presbyterian Church, the mournful fact is patent, that the congregations which that church embraces are more and more succumbing to its baleful influence. The ministers who are opposed to the unscriptural movement are, many of them at least, indisposed to throw themselves into opposition to its onward rush. They are unwilling to make an issue with their people upon this question. They are reluctant to characterize the employment of instrumental music in public worship as a sin. But a sin it is, if there be any force in the argument which opposes it. The people ought to be taught that in using it they rebel against the law of Christ, their King.

It bodes ill for the church that this subject is now so often treated in a flippant and even jocular manner. The question of the use of instrumental music in the public worship of God's house is, for example, sometimes placed upon the same foot with that in regard to the use of tobacco. Both questions are scouted as equally illegitimate and equally trivial. Is tobacco ever mentioned in the Word of God? Is it forgotten that a private habit of an individual is a vastly different thing from an action which modifies the public, solemn singing of God's praise by a congregation of professed worshippers? Such levity partakes of profanity. It makes a mock of holy things. The indulgence of this temper by our church courts will betoken the departure of our glory. It is not less than shocking to suppose that the church can make light of a subject about which God's jealousy has smoked, and his anger has broken out into a consuming flame. If she will employ instruments of music, let her at least refrain from fiddling while many of her children are mourning over what they feel to be the corruption of her worship and the decay of her spirituality. Nero fiddled while Rome was burning, and Belshazzar was desecrating the vessels of God's sanctuary in the midst of revelry when the mystic hand wrote on the wall of his palace the sentence of doom.

Those of us who protest against this revolution in Presbyterian worship are by some pitied, by others ridiculed, and by others still denounced as fanatics. If we are, we share the company of an innumerable host of fanatics extending from the day of Pentecost to the middle of the nineteenth century. We refuse not to be classed, although consciously unworthy of the honor, with apostles, martyrs and reformers. But neither were they mad, nor are we. We "speak the words of truth and soberness." Mindful of the apostolic injunction, "Prove all things," we submit arguments derived from Scripture, from the formularies of our church and from the *consensus* of Christ's people, and respectfully invoke for them the attention of our brethren. We call upon them to examine these arguments, and either disprove or adopt them. But should they be dismissed without notice, and our faithful remonstrances be unheeded, we humbly, but earnestly, warn the church of the evil and bitter consequences which will, we verily believe, be entailed by that corruption of public worship which has been pointed out; and against it, in the name of the framers of our venerable standards, in the name of the reformers, divines and martyrs of the Presbyterian Church, in the name of Christ's true witnesses in the centuries of the past, in the name of the inspired apostles, and, above all, in the name of our glorious King and Head, we erect our solemn **PROTEST.**

www.ingramcontent.com/pod-product-compliance
Lightning Source LLC
Chambersburg PA
CBHW021727220426
43662CB00008B/739